5 Big Ideas

FOR LEADING A

High Reliability School

ROBERT J. MARZANO   PHILIP B. WARRICK   MARIO I. ACOSTA

555 North Morton Street
Bloomington, IN 47404
800.733.6786 (toll free) / 812.336.7700
FAX: 812.336.7790

email: info@MarzanoResources.com
MarzanoResources.com

Printed in the United States of America

Library of Congress Cataloging-in-Publication Data

Names: Marzano, Robert J., author. | Warrick, Philip B., author. | Acosta,
    Mario I., author.
Title: Five big ideas for leading a high reliability school / Robert J.
    Marzano, Philip B. Warrick, Mario I. Acosta.
Description: Bloomington, IN : Marzano Resources, [2024] | Includes
    bibliographical references and index.
Identifiers: LCCN 2023038763 (print) | LCCN 2023038764 (ebook) | ISBN
    9781943360826 (paperback) | ISBN 9781943360833 (ebook)
Subjects: LCSH: Educational leadership. | School management and
    organization. | Education--Research. | Academic achievement.
Classification: LCC LB2806 .M37134 2024 (print) | LCC LB2806 (ebook) |
    DDC 371.2/011--dc23/eng/20230913
LC record available at https://lccn.loc.gov/2023038763
LC ebook record available at https://lccn.loc.gov/2023038764

Production Team
President and Publisher: Douglas M. Rife
Associate Publishers: Todd Brakke and Kendra Slayton
Editorial Director: Laurel Hecker
Art Director: Rian Anderson
Copy Chief: Jessi Finn
Developmental Editor: Laurel Hecker
Copy Editor: Mark Hain
Proofreader: Sarah Ludwig
Text and Cover Designer: Laura Cox
Acquisitions Editor: Hilary Goff
Assistant Acquisitions Editor: Elijah Oates
Content Development Specialist: Amy Rubenstein
Associate Editor: Sarah Ludwig
Editorial Assistant: Anne Marie Watkins

Table of Contents

About the Authors

Robert J. Marzano, PhD, is cofounder and chief academic officer of Marzano Resources in Denver, Colorado. During his fifty years in the field of education, he has worked with educators as a speaker and trainer and has authored more than fifty books and two hundred articles on topics such as instruction, assessment, writing and implementing standards, cognition, effective leadership, and school intervention. His books include *The New Art and Science of Teaching, Leaders of Learning, Making Classroom Assessments Reliable and Valid, The Classroom Strategies Series, Managing the Inner World of Teaching, A Handbook for High Reliability Schools, A Handbook for Personalized Competency-Based Education*, and *The Highly Engaged Classroom*. His practical translations of the most current research and theory into classroom strategies are known internationally and are widely practiced by both teachers and administrators.

Dr. Marzano received a bachelor's degree from Iona College in New York, a master's degree from Seattle University, and a doctorate from the University of Washington.

To learn more about Dr. Marzano, visit www.marzanoresources.com.

Philip B. Warrick, EdD, spent the first twenty-five years of his education career as a teacher, assistant principal, principal, and superintendent and has experience leading schools in the states of Nebraska and Texas. He was named 1998 Nebraska Outstanding New Principal of the Year and was the 2005 Nebraska State High School Principal of the Year. In 2003, he was one of the initial participants in the Nebraska Educational Leadership Institute, conducted by the Gallup Corporation at Gallup University in Omaha. In 2008, Dr. Warrick was hired as the campus principal at Round Rock High School in Round Rock, Texas. In 2010, he was invited to be an inaugural participant in the Texas Principals' Visioning Institute, where he collaborated with other principals from the state to develop a vision for effective practices in Texas schools. In 2011, Dr. Warrick joined the Solution Tree–Marzano Resources team and works as an author and global consultant in the areas of High Reliability School leadership, instruction and instructional coaching, assessment, grading, and collaborative teaming.

Dr. Warrick earned a bachelor of science from Chadron State College in Chadron, Nebraska, and his master's and doctoral degrees from the University of Nebraska–Lincoln.

To learn more about Dr. Warrick's work, follow @pbwarrick on Twitter.

Mario I. Acosta, EdD, spent twenty years of his educational career as a teacher, instructional coach, assistant principal, academic director, and principal leading schools with diverse profiles in the state of Texas. He was named the Texas 2022 Principal of the Year while principal at Westwood High School in Austin, a U.S. News & World Report top-fifty campus and member of the High Reliability Schools Network.

Dr. Acosta has had success in leading schools of all sizes, with students and teachers from a variety of backgrounds, communities, and socioeconomic statuses. He has led school turnaround in high-poverty schools in Texas at both the middle and high school levels, which yielded immediate and significant growth in student achievement data. Furthermore, under his leadership, Westwood High School was recognized as a top 1 percent campus in the United States for its academic achievement and college and career readiness.

In 2022, Dr. Acosta joined the Solution Tree–Marzano Resources team and works as an author and national presenter. He specializes in campus-level implementation of effective campus culture, High Reliability Schools, professional learning communities (PLCs), instructional improvement, response to intervention, effective teaching strategies for English learners (ELs), and standards-referenced reporting. As a High Reliability School certifier, Dr. Acosta works with K–12 schools and districts across the United States as they progress through the various levels of certification. He also serves as a professor at the University of Texas at Austin, where he prepares students in the educational leadership master's degree program to become school leaders.

Dr. Acosta holds a doctorate in educational administration from the University of Texas at Austin and a superintendent certification in the state of Texas. He earned a bachelor's degree in mathematics from the University of Texas at Austin and a master's degree from Lamar University in Beaumont, Texas.

To learn more about Dr. Acosta's work, follow @marioacosta31 on Twitter.

To book Robert J. Marzano, Philip B. Warrick, or Mario I. Acosta for professional development, contact pd@MarzanoResources.com.

Introduction

The High Reliability Schools Framework

The High Reliability Schools (HRS) framework is a five-level framework schools can use to gauge their effectiveness with respect to practices that have emerged from the research literature on improvement of student outcomes (see figure I.1). The framework was first introduced in *A Handbook for High Reliability Schools* (Marzano, Warrick, & Simms, 2014). Since then, over 1,600 schools have participated in the process to certify their performance on those elements that constitute the HRS framework. While the HRS framework is for schools, it is an adaptation of research and theory on high reliability organizations (HROs) in the business sector.

Level 5	Competency-Based Education
Level 4	Standards-Referenced Reporting
Level 3	Guaranteed and Viable Curriculum
Level 2	Effective Teaching in Every Classroom
Level 1	Safe, Supportive, and Collaborative Culture

Source: Adapted from Marzano et al., 2014.

Figure I.1: HRS levels.

The Nature of High Reliability Organizations

The concept of a high reliability organization has been at the vanguard of effective practice in a variety of venues. G. Thomas Bellamy, Lindy Crawford, Laura Marshall, and Gail Coulter (2005) explained, "the literature on HROs describes how organizations operate when accidents or failures are simply too significant to be tolerated, where failures make headlines" (p. 385). In other words, when "the public expects fail-safe performance" (Bellamy et al., 2005, p. 385), organizations should adopt a high reliability perspective. Examples include toxic chemical manufacturing, nuclear power plants, electric power grids, air traffic control systems, prisoner confinement and transportation, and commercial aircraft maintenance.

Becoming a high reliability organization in any arena is not a simple process. As Karl Weick, Kathleen Sutcliffe, and David Obstfeld (1999) explained, high reliability organizations "take a variety of extraordinary steps in pursuit of error free performance" (p. 84). Bellamy and his colleagues (2005) noted that high reliability organizations are not products of serendipity. Rather, they require thoughtful planning and execution:

> The study of HROs has evolved through empirical investigation of catastrophic accidents, near misses, and organizations that succeed despite very trying and dangerous circumstances. Launched by Perrow's (1984) analysis of the nuclear accident at Three Mile Island, the literature evolved through discussions of whether such accidents are inevitable, as Perrow suggested, or might be avoided through strategies used by organizations that operate successfully in high-risk conditions (Bierly & Spender, 1995; Roberts, 1990). Although there are some similarities between this literature and research on organizational effectiveness and quality improvement, HROs "have been treated as exotic outliers in mainstream organizational theory because of their unique potentials for catastrophic consequences and interactively complex technology (Weick et al., 1999, p. 81). (Bellamy et al., 2005, p. 385)

It is important for educators to note that, while high reliability organizations aspire to error-free performance, they are certainly not error free. Indeed, Bellamy and colleagues (2005) emphasized the fact that all organizations make mistakes, but "what distinguishes HROs is not the absence of errors but the ability to contain their effects so they do not escalate into significant failures" (p. 385).

In contrast to the enthusiasm for operating as a high reliability organization in the business world, K–12 schools do not typically aspire to this status. To explain the lack of emphasis on high reliability procedures in K–12 education, one might postulate that schools do not lend themselves to this type of structure; since the concept was designed for the business world, it does not apply in the world of education. However, there is nothing inherent in a school's structure or its focus on teaching K–12 students that would inhibit it from becoming a high reliability organization. Indeed, there has been a largely ignored discussion in the education literature for decades regarding the adoption of high reliability protocols. For example, in 1995, Sam Stringfield described the outcomes that would qualify a school as operating from a high reliability perspective. One might legitimately say that Stringfield was a pioneer in advocating that K–12 schools operate as high reliability organizations.

To function as a high reliability organization, a school must determine "the right work" in which it must engage. "The right work" is a term Richard Elmore (2003) popularized when he noted that it is not how much schools do that distinguishes effective from ineffective, but what they choose to work on. Specifically, in a study commissioned by the National Governors Association (NGA), Elmore (2003) concluded:

> Knowing the right thing to do is the central problem of school improvement. Holding schools accountable for their performance depends on having people in the schools with the knowledge, skill, and judgment to make the improvements that will increase student performance. (p. 9)

Elmore made the case that many educators suffer from the misperception that schools fail because teachers and administrators don't work hard enough. In contrast, Elmore proposes that low-performing schools' mistakes are not rooted in their lack of effort and motivation, but in poor decisions regarding what to work on. Educators in low-performing schools do, in fact, work hard, but they focus on "the wrong work" as opposed to "the right work." The central question, then, for a school seeking high reliability status is, What is the right work for us?

The History of Trying to Identify the Right Work

One can make a case that the history of trying to identify the right work in U.S. schools started in the late 1970s when researchers in the U.S. launched large-scale coordinated efforts to determine the factors that defined "effective schools," a term Lawrence Lezotte (1989) popularized in his article "School Improvement Based on the Effective Schools Research." We review this research later in this introduction, but we take the position that efforts to identify the right work actually date back at least to the middle of the 20th century and were fueled by a desire to determine the equity and effectiveness of U.S. schools. In the postwar era of the 1950s and 1960s, people in the United States became more aware of poverty, racism, and unequal educational opportunity as activists struggled to bring these issues into popular consciousness (Madaus, Airasian, & Kellaghan, 1980). Efforts to identify and respond to issues of unequal educational opportunity, especially those that affected minority-group children, directly influenced the school effectiveness movement. It was in this cultural environment that President Lyndon Johnson began his war on poverty through the Civil Rights Act of 1964. That legislation directed the Commissioner of Education to survey the availability of educational opportunity nationally. The act specifically noted that:

> The Commissioner shall conduct a survey and make a report to the President and Congress . . . concerning the *lack of availability of equal educational opportunities* [emphasis added] for individuals by reason of race, color, religion, or national origin in public institutions. (as cited in Madaus et al., 1980, p. 12)

While the legislation did not explicitly state that opportunities to learn were not equal for all students, the implication was strong in its wording. Madaus and colleagues (1980) explained:

> It is not clear why Congress ordered the commissioner to conduct the survey, although the phrase "concerning the lack of availability of educational opportunities" implies that Congress believed that inequalities in opportunities did exist, and that documenting these differences could provide a useful legal and political tool to overcome future oppositions to school reform. (p. 12)

According to Frederick Mosteller and Daniel P. Moynihan (1972), the man selected to head the team of researchers conducting the survey, James Coleman, openly expected the study to reveal significant disparities in quality when comparing the education provided to Black students versus White students. Mosteller and Moynihan interpreted this as evidence that Coleman already had conclusions in mind when he began the study.

The study Coleman and his researchers ultimately executed involved over 640,000 students in grades 1, 3, 6, 9, and 12; the study grouped students into six ethnic and cultural categories. All students took parallel achievement tests and aptitude tests. The study also surveyed some 60,000 teachers in over 4,000 schools in detail about their background and training. It was the largest examination of public education undertaken to that point.

The findings from the study were published in 1966 in a report titled *Equality of Educational Opportunity* (commonly referred to as "the Coleman report"). Educators and policymakers generally interpreted the report's overall findings as a condemnation of schools' inability to overcome differences in student achievement due to their home environment. One of the study's main conclusions was that schools bring little influence to bear on students' achievement independent of their backgrounds and social context. In other words, schools do not have much effect, meaning that "the inequalities imposed on children by their home, neighborhood, and peer environments are the inequalities with which they confront adult life at the end of school" (Coleman et al., 1966, p. 325). Madaus and colleagues (1980) concluded that the Coleman report produced two major perceptions about K–12 education in the United States. First, it severely damaged the belief that schools could equalize the disparity in social and environmental factors that caused student achievement gaps. Second, it gave the impression that differences or changes in what schools do have little to no impact on student achievement. The report found that schools account for only about 10 percent of the variances in student achievement—the other 90 percent was accounted for by student background characteristics—and this statistic was widely publicized.

A few years later, Christopher Jencks and colleagues (1972) published the report *Inequality: A Reassessment of the Effect of Family and Schooling in America*, which reanalyzed data from the Coleman report. Their reported findings included the following.

- Schools do little to lessen the gap between rich and poor students.
- Schools do little to lessen the gap between more and less abled students.
- Student achievement is primarily a function of one factor—the background of the student.
- There is little evidence that education reform can improve the influence a school has on student achievement. (Marzano, 2001, p. 2)

Given that the findings from the Coleman report and Jencks and colleagues' reanalysis were widely publicized, it is easy to see why many educators and noneducators developed the perspective that school improvement is a losing proposition. Logically, it would be a waste of energy to attempt to improve schools if schools have little chance of overcoming the influence of students' background characteristics.

It was this backdrop of assumed school ineffectiveness that led researchers in the 1970s to search for concrete factors that did render schools effective. The Michigan School Improvement Program (MSIP), housed at Michigan State University's School of Education, helped organize some of these early studies, which collectively became known as the school effectiveness movement. Table I.1 briefly summarizes some of the better-known studies within this movement. For a detailed analysis of these studies, see *A New Era of School Reform* (Marzano, 2001).

By the early 1980s, the initial school effectiveness movement was coming to an end and was replaced by studies whose aim was to synthesize large bodies of research in the hopes of identifying generalizations and principles that could be applied to all schools. Table I.2 (page 6) describes some of the more prominent synthesis studies conducted in the 1980s and 1990s.

Table I.1: Well-Known Studies on School Effectiveness

Klitgaard and Hall	In their study *Are There Unusually Effective Schools?*, Robert Klitgaard and George Hall (1975) analyzed multiyear test data from 788 schools in Michigan and New York. Their study was not so much focused on the specific characteristics of effective schools as it was on demonstrating that there are schools that generate levels of student learning well beyond statistical expectations.
Brookover and Colleagues	A study by Wilbur Brookover and his colleagues (Brookover et al., 1978; Brookover et al., 1979) involved sixty-eight elementary schools. Variables used to predict student achievement included overall school climate, teacher satisfaction, parental involvement, teaching practices, student perceptions of the school in general and opportunities it presented them, teacher and administrator expectations regarding students' abilities to learn, as well as input variables such as student socioeconomic status, school size, teacher qualifications, and school resources. One of the major findings of the study was that these factors in a school interact in ways unique to each school, yet in aggregate account for a great deal of the variance in student achievement.
Edmonds	Ron Edmonds had a number of influential publications in the 1970s and early 1980s (Edmonds, 1979a, 1979b, 1979c, 1981a, 1981b; Edmonds & Frederiksen, 1979). He operationalized the definition of an effective school as one that closes the achievement gap between students from low socioeconomic backgrounds and those from high socioeconomic backgrounds. He is probably most remembered for his identification of five school-level variables that are highly correlated with student achievement: (1) strong administrative leadership, (2) high expectations for student achievement, (3) an orderly atmosphere conducive to learning, (4) an emphasis on basic skill acquisition, and (5) frequent monitoring of student progress. These became known as "the correlates."
Rutter	Michael Rutter and his colleagues conducted a study of secondary schools in London which culminated in the book *Fifteen Thousand Hours: Secondary Schools and Their Effects on Children* (Rutter, Maughan, Mortimore, & Ouston, 1979). They identified the following factors as critical to a school's effectiveness: (1) emphasis on academics, (2) teaching behavior, (3) use of rewards and punishments, (4) degree of student responsibility, (5) staff stability, and (6) staff organization.
Outlier Studies	A number of studies that were done in the heyday of the school effectiveness movement can be loosely referred to as *outlier studies* (Scheerens & Bosker, 1997). The general methodology in this approach is to identify groups of schools with similar student demographics. Within the school effectiveness research, the primary demographic of interest was whether students came from low socioeconomic status backgrounds. Researchers rank-ordered schools in the studies by student achievement on large-scale external assessments. Researchers then analyzed the programs and practices of high-achieving versus low-achieving schools to determine what differentiated them. Stewart C. Purkey and Marshall S. Smith (1982, 1983) summarized the general findings from these studies, noting the following characteristics as common to high-achieving schools: (1) good discipline, (2) teachers' high expectations regarding student achievement, and (3) effective leadership by the school administrators.
Case Studies	Case studies represent a significant set of research efforts to identify those school-level factors that have a relationship with student achievement. These studies consider a small set of schools in depth. Researchers usually organize schools into groups of high achieving versus low achieving based on outcome measures. Researchers do extensive site visits and collect a variety of data, such as classroom observational data, surveys, interviews, and the like. Influential case studies were conducted by George Weber (1971), Richard L. Venezky and Linda F. Winfield (1979), Beverly Caffee Glenn and Taylor McLean (1981), and Brookover and Lezotte (1979). In aggregate, these studies identified success factors such as strong leadership, orderliness, high expectations, frequent evaluation, cooperation, clear academic goals, and effective staff development.

Source: Adapted from Marzano, 2001.

Table I.2: Synthesis Studies of School Effectiveness

Walberg	Herbert J. Walberg (1980, 1984) used the Cobb-Douglas function, a mathematical model from economics, to synthesize the findings from some three thousand studies. He developed what he referred to as the *productivity model.* Walberg's ultimate conclusion was that the variables that can best predict student achievement fall into three broad categories: student aptitude, instruction, and environment.
Bloom	In 1984, Benjamin S. Bloom (1984a, 1984b) published two articles that demonstrated to K–12 educators the practical utility of conducting a meta-analysis that synthesized findings in the form of a standardized mean difference, popularly known as an effect size. He conducted a meta-analysis on tutoring and found that it had an effect size of 2.00. He explained that this means that the average student under tutoring was about two standard deviations above the average student in the control classes (that is, the average tutored student was above the ninety-eighth percentile of the students in the control classes). This sparked research interest in trying to find school- or teacher-level factors that could match this high effect size.
Fraser, Walberg, Welch, and Hattie	In 1987, the *International Journal of Educational Research* devoted an issue to a summary of the effects of school- and classroom-level variables on student achievement (Fraser, Walberg, Welch, & Hattie, 1987). It highlighted three sets of findings. The first set of findings utilized Walberg's productivity model to synthesize the results of 2,575 individual studies. The overall conclusion of this section was that the following variables appear to substitute, compensate, or trade off for one another at diminishing rates of return in terms of student achievement: ability, development, motivation, quantity of instruction, and quality of instruction. The second set of findings involved a synthesis of 134 meta-analyses that were based on 7,827 studies and 22,155 effect sizes. Seven general factors emerged as significantly related to student achievement: (1) school factors, (2) social factors, (3) instructor factors, (4) instructional factors, (5) pupil factors, (6) methods of instruction, and (7) learning strategies. The third set of findings was specific to science achievement. It identified the following student-level factors that were related to science achievement: (1) ability, (2) motivation, (3) quality of instruction, (4) quantity of instruction, (5) class environment, (6) home environment, and (7) frequency of television viewing (which was negatively related to student learning).
Hattie	John Hattie was one of the coauthors of Barry J. Fraser, Herbert J. Walberg, Wayne W. Welch, and John A. Hattie's (1987) study described in the previous row. In 1992, he republished these findings along with some previously unarticulated generalizations. One was that any systematic and sustained attempt to improve schools typically shows up as enhanced student achievement. Another is that the typical effect size is about 0.40. In 1996, Hattie, John Biggs, and Nola Purdie synthesized fifty-one studies of instructional practices involving 270 effect sizes and identified four types of instructional practices: (1) unistructural tasks, (2) multistructural tasks, (3) relational tasks, and (4) extended abstract tasks. Since this effort, Hattie has continued to synthesize the educational research, resulting in a 2009 publication that identified 138 rank-ordered variables, a 2012 publication that resulted in 150 rank-ordered variables, and a 2015 publication that resulted in 195 rank-ordered variables.
Lipsey and Wilson	In 1993, Mark W. Lipsey and David B. Wilson conducted a meta-analysis of 302 studies that cut across education and psychology. They analyzed 16,902 effect sizes and found the mean to be 0.50. Some of the most enduring findings dealt with the differences in effect sizes between various types of studies. They found no statistically significant difference in effect sizes between studies that were rated high in methodological quality versus studies that were rated low in methodological quality. Neither were there statistically significant differences in effect sizes between studies that used random assignment to experimental and control groups and those that used nonrandom assignment to groups. However, there was a 0.29 statistically significant differential between effect sizes that were computed from comparisons of experimental versus control groups and those from one-group, pre- and post-test designs, with the latter having the larger effect size.
Wang, Haertel, and Walberg	In 1993, Margaret C. Wang, Geneva D. Haertel, and Herbert J. Walberg published an overall synthesis of three previous synthesis efforts. The first of these encompassed 3,700 citations and identified 228 variables. The second study of the triad surveyed 134 education experts who reviewed the 228 variables and ranked them. The third effort used the results of 136 meta-analyses. Data from these three efforts were translated into a common metric, which the researchers referred to as a T-score, and then the T-scores were combined to create a list of thirty variables that were organized into six theoretical constructs: (1) student characteristic; (2) classroom practices; (3) home and community educational context; (4) design and delivery of curriculum and instruction; (5) school demographics, culture, climate, policies, and practices; and (6) state and district governance and organization.
Scheerens and Bosker	In a series of studies, Jaap Scheerens and Roel Bosker (Bosker, 1992; Bosker & Witziers, 1995, 1996; Scheerens, 1992; Scheerens & Bosker, 1997) conducted a meta-analysis of international research on nine factors that came out of the school effectiveness literature: (1) cooperation, (2) school climate, (3) monitoring, (4) content coverage, (5) homework, (6) time, (7) parental involvement, (8) pressure to achieve, and (9) leadership. Of particular note in their study was that they were some of the first researchers to use hierarchical linear modeling (HLM) as the tool for statistical analysis.

Source: Adapted from Marzano, 2001.

Since the turn of the millennium, synthesis studies have continued in an effort to generate a definitive list of the right work for schools. However, the vast majority of these studies have focused on synthesizing the research on specific factors like school culture (Bektaş, Çoğaltay, Karadağ, & Yusuf, 2015), leadership (Waters & Cameron, 2007), and the like. To date, only the efforts of John Hattie and his colleagues have continued on the path of synthesizing the research on multiple factors.

Hattie's meta-analytic studies are unprecedented in their breadth and depth; these studies span decades of research and synthesize tens of thousands of quantitative relationships expressed as effect sizes. From 2009 to 2015, Hattie published three related versions of a list of factors ranked in terms of their relationship to student academic achievement. *Visible Learning* (2009) identified 138 factors, *Visible Learning for Teachers* (2012) expanded the list of factors to 150, and "The Applicability of Visible Learning to Higher Education" (2015) expanded the list to 195 factors. Table I.3 lists the top ten factors in Hattie's studies across these three publications.

Table I.3: Summary of Hattie's Top Ten Factors Across Three Studies

Rank	2009 Total Factors = 138	2012 Total Factors = 150	2015 Total Factors = 195
1	Student self-reported grades (1.44)	Student self-reported grades and expectations (1.44)	Teacher estimates of achievement (1.62)
2	Piagetian programs (1.28; Jordan & Brownlee, 1981)	Piagetian programs (1.28)	Collective teacher efficacy (1.57)
3	Formative evaluation (0.90)	Response to intervention (RTI; 1.07)	Self-reported grades (1.33)
4	Micro-teaching (0.88)	Teacher credibility (0.90)	Piagetian programs (1.28)
5	Acceleration (0.88)	Formative evaluation (0.90)	Conceptual change programs (1.16)
6	Improved classroom behavior (0.80)	Micro-teaching (0.88)	RTI (1.07)
7	Comprehensive interventions for students with learning disabilities (0.77)	Class discussion (0.82)	Teacher credibility (0.90)
8	Teacher clarity (0.75)	Comprehensive interventions for students with learning disabilities (0.77)	Micro-teaching (0.88)
9	Reciprocal teaching (0.74)	Teacher clarity (0.75)	Cognitive task analysis (0.87)
10	Feedback (0.73)	Feedback (0.75)	Classroom discussion (0.82)

Source: Adapted from Marzano & Eaker, 2020.

At an intuitive level, it seems reasonable to identify the right work in a school by selecting factors at the top of Hattie's lists and working down. However, there are a number of reasons why this approach is not viable. Probably the most important problem is that educators are likely to ignore factors that are necessary but not sufficient conditions for effective schooling. For example, consider the factor of decreasing disruptive behavior in the school and classrooms. While it is fairly obvious that decreasing disruptions is foundational to effective schooling, it ranks 103 (Hattie, 2015). Similarly, reducing students' levels of anxiety ranks 97, and enhancing students' motivation ranks 74 (Hattie, 2015). Other factors that are important to effective schooling but appear far from the top of Hattie's lists include early intervention (130), school culture (150), and teacher immediacy (160). As these examples illustrate, many of the factors that are foundational to effective schooling are found rather low on Hattie's lists.

A second reason for not starting at the top of Hattie's lists (or any other lists) of effect sizes and progressing down is that there is nothing inherent in a large effect size that indicates the variable it represents is more important to schooling than a variable with a smaller effect size. As explained by researchers Gene V. Glass, Barry McGaw, and Mary Lee Smith (1981):

> There is no wisdom whatsoever in attempting to associate regions of the effect size metric with descriptive adjectives such as "small," "moderate," "large," and the like. Dissociated from a context of decision and comparative value, there is little inherent value to an effect size of 3.5 or .2. Depending on what benefits can be achieved at what cost, an effect size of 2.0 might be "poor" and one of .1 might be "good." (p. 104)

Researcher Mark W. Lipsey and colleagues (2012) explained that those trying to draw inferences from effect sizes must think in terms of *practical significance*, which involves a comparison with typical expectations. The researchers noted:

> Practical significance is not an inherent characteristic of the numbers and statistics that result from intervention research—it is something that must be judged in some context of application. To interpret the practical significance of an intervention effect, therefore, it is necessary to invoke an appropriate frame of reference external to its statistical representation. (Lipsey et al., 2012, p. 26)

A final reason why lists of variables rank-ordered by effect sizes should not be interpreted in too literal a manner is that the results of meta-analytic studies commonly change over time. This is not a criticism of Hattie's work or of meta-analytic research in general. Variation in rank order of variables is simply inherent in the approach. Over time, meta-analytic researchers integrate more studies into existing sets of findings, change their definitions of factors, add factors, and even exclude factors. For example, consider the factor of student self-reported grades, which Hattie ranked first in the 2009 study. In the 2012 study, this factor was still ranked first, but Hattie changed its description to *student self-reported grades and expectations*. Collective teacher efficacy is another example of this variation; Hattie ranked this variable second in the 2015 study even though it did not appear in either of the two previous studies. Finally, the factor of quality of teaching was ranked fifty-sixth in the 2009 study and fifty-seventh in the 2012 study. However, this factor disappeared from the list in the 2015 study.

The HRS Version of the Right Work

From the discussion above, it is clear that the right work for schools must be identified in the context of both quantitative research and the practical reality of how schools operate. In designing the HRS framework, we attempted to marry the research since the beginning of the school effectiveness movement with the practical realities of managing and improving a school as experienced by school leaders. The right work as defined in the HRS framework is represented by twenty-five variables distributed over five levels. They are depicted in figure I.2.

Level	Leading Indicators
Level 1: Safe, Supportive, and Collaborative Culture	1.1—The faculty and staff perceive the school environment as safe, supportive, and orderly. 1.2—Students, parents, and the community perceive the school environment as safe, supportive, and orderly. 1.3—Teachers have formal roles in the decision-making process regarding school initiatives. 1.4—Teacher teams and collaborative groups regularly interact to address common issues regarding curriculum, assessment, instruction, and the achievement of all students. 1.5—Teachers and staff have formal ways to provide input regarding the optimal functioning of the school. 1.6—Students, parents, and the community have formal ways to provide input regarding the optimal functioning of the school. 1.7—The school acknowledges the success of the whole school as well as individuals within the school. 1.8—The school manages its fiscal, operational, and technological resources in a way that directly supports teachers.
Level 2: Effective Teaching in Every Classroom	2.1—The school communicates a clear vision as to how teachers should address instruction. 2.2—The school supports teachers to continually enhance their pedagogical skills through reflection and professional growth plans. 2.3—The school is aware of and monitors predominant instructional practices. 2.4—The school provides teachers with clear, ongoing evaluations of their pedagogical strengths and weaknesses that are based on multiple sources of data and are consistent with student achievement data. 2.5—The school provides teachers with job-embedded professional development that is directly related to their instructional growth goals. 2.6—Teachers have opportunities to observe and discuss effective teaching.
Level 3: Guaranteed and Viable Curriculum	3.1—The school curriculum and accompanying assessments adhere to state and district standards. 3.2—The school curriculum is focused enough that teachers can adequately address it in the time they have available. 3.3—All students have the opportunity to learn the critical content of the curriculum. 3.4—The school establishes clear and measurable goals that are focused on critical needs regarding improving overall student achievement at the school level. 3.5—The school analyzes, interprets, and uses data to regularly monitor progress toward school achievement goals. 3.6—The school establishes appropriate school- and classroom-level programs and practices to help students meet individual achievement goals when data indicate interventions are needed.
Level 4: Standards-Referenced Reporting	4.1—The school establishes clear and measurable goals focused on critical needs regarding improving achievement of individual students. 4.2—The school analyzes, interprets, and uses data to regularly monitor progress toward achievement goals for individual students.
Level 5: Competency-Based Education	5.1—Students move on to the next level of the curriculum for any subject area only after they have demonstrated competence at the previous level. 5.2—The school schedule accommodates students moving at a pace appropriate to their situation and needs. 5.3—The school affords students who have demonstrated competency levels greater than those articulated in the system immediate opportunities to begin work on advanced content or career paths of interest.

Source: Adapted from Marzano et al., 2014.

Figure I.2: The "right work" as defined in the HRS framework.

Of course, any list of factors purporting to be the right work for schools comes from a specific perspective and has specific biases. This generalization certainly applies to the list in figure I.2 (page 9). Its foundational perspectives and biases are explored in books like *What Works in Schools* (Marzano, 2003), *Formative Assessment and Standards-Based Grading* (Marzano, 2010), *Leading a High Reliability School* (Marzano, Warrick, Rains, & DuFour, 2018), *Improving Teacher Development and Evaluation* (Marzano, Rains, & Warrick, 2021), and *Professional Learning Communities at Work® and High Reliability Schools* (Eaker & Marzano, 2020), to name a few. Given this reality, some schools and districts with whom we have worked augment the list of twenty-five HRS indicators by adding others that are more specific to their situations. This is a powerful approach with which we wholeheartedly agree.

The twenty-five variables (that is, indicators) exist within five different levels. These levels represent our strong theoretical stance as to factors that are foundational for schools to be effective and those elements that build up from the support provided by the elements below them. Level 1 of the HRS framework focuses on developing a safe, supportive, and collaborative culture. This is the foundational level because these indicators deal with basic human needs. When students and teachers don't feel safe at school, their focus is diverted from student learning. A culture that supports agency and collaboration likewise empowers students and teachers to grow both individually and collectively.

Level 2 of the framework addresses effective teaching. The quality of teaching to which students are exposed has a significant influence on their achievement. An effective school should have teacher improvement built into its structure. This level of the model helps teachers develop their pedagogical skills by engaging in deliberate practice in specific strategies from the school's explicit model of instruction.

Level 3 ensures that schools have a guaranteed and viable curriculum. A *guaranteed* curriculum is one for which every student in a given course or at a given grade level has the opportunity to learn the same content, regardless of the teacher to whom they are assigned. A *viable* curriculum is one that is focused enough that teachers have the necessary time and resources to teach it.

Level 4 concerns the implementation of standards-referenced reporting. Instead of merely reporting an omnibus grade in a subject, a standards-referenced reporting system identifies each individual student's current status on specific topics. It also reports growth over time in reference to those topics.

Level 5 addresses the shift to full competency-based education (CBE) in which students advance to the next level of content as soon as they demonstrate mastery of the topics at their current level. This is in sharp contrast to a traditional system in which students must spend a specific amount of time in a class or course before they can matriculate to the next level of content.

The twenty-five factors that make up the levels of the HRS framework are embodied in a series of *leading indicators* that describe the actions a school takes to increase its effectiveness. By continually comparing the results of those actions to benchmarks called *lagging indicators*, a school can monitor the effectiveness of its efforts, and then detect and recover from problems before they become significant issues.

The Five Big Ideas for Leading a High Reliability School

Over the years since Robert J. Marzano, Philip B. Warrick, and Julia A. Simms (2014) first introduced the HRS model, it has become evident that schools do not reach high reliability status without strong leaders. It has also become evident that the success of a school to this end is, at least in part, dependent on the extent to which school leadership is implicitly or explicitly aware of five "big ideas." Those big ideas are as follows.

1. Becoming an HRS is a measurement process.
2. Certain levels of the HRS framework have a more direct relationship to student achievement as measured by external tests than others.
3. Schools must tailor programs and practices to their specific needs.
4. Without adequate focus and energy, even effective programs and practices will start to degrade.
5. Standards-referenced reporting and competency-based education are at the top of the HRS framework because of their magnitude of change and their focus on equity.

These five big ideas are the focus of this book.

In This Book

In the remainder of this book, readers will find in-depth discussions of each of the five big ideas in the context of the HRS process. We devote one chapter to each big idea. Each chapter begins with a discussion of the research and theory supporting the big idea and then presents examples of how that big idea manifests in K–12 schools. At the end of each chapter, we summarize its key insights and suggest actions readers may be motivated to take in response. Following the epilogue, an appendix contains tools for leaders to assess their school's level of performance on each leading indicator and set lagging indicators.

Educators and researchers in the United States have been attempting to determine what makes a school effective in terms of enhancing student learning for many decades. The HRS framework pulls from this vast reservoir of information to create a system schools can use to become high reliability organizations. Striving to function as a high reliability organization is not unusual in the business world, but is relatively new to the world of K–12 education. We feel strongly that the indicators that comprise each level of the HRS framework represent "the right work" for schools, and our experience implementing this framework has revealed that school leaders' cognizance of certain truths about the process bears heavily on the success of that work. This book will ensure that you are prepared to lead your school in operating as a high reliability organization.

Big Idea 1

Becoming a High Reliability School Is a Measurement Process

A common misconception about the HRS certification process is that it is an intervention or a specific program a school adopts to become better. It is certainly true that the HRS framework *involves* interventions in the form of programs and practices designed to produce specific outcomes. Indeed, the first step of the HRS process involves identifying programs and practices that address each leading indicator. Such programs and practices might already be in place in a school, or the school might have to identify or develop new programs and practices. In effect, the HRS process is *intervention agnostic*. It does not require schools to use specific programs or practices but does require schools to determine the effectiveness of the programs and practices they use now or will use in the future. While the HRS process involves interventions, it is fundamentally a measurement process. To understand HRS as a measurement process, it is useful to first consider the HRS certification process.

The HRS Certification Process

Speaking in nontechnical terms, one might say that measurement involves collecting, analyzing, and interpreting data. To achieve official HRS certification at a given level of the framework, a school must submit its data and the interpretations accompanying it to a team of reviewers at Marzano Resources. However, school leaders, faculty, and staff can also engage in the HRS measurement process themselves. In either situation, there are five steps to which a school must attend.

1. **Make sure there are programs and practices in place for each leading indicator:** For many leading indicators, schools typically find that they already have programs and practices in place. If they do not, then the first thing the school must do is identify and implement programs and practices that directly address the leading indicator. To illustrate, consider indicator 2.1, "The school communicates a clear vision as to how teachers should address instruction." The concrete practice that is necessary to fulfill this leading indicator is to have an explicit model of instruction in place that all teachers are aware of. If a school finds that it does not have such a model, then its first order of business is to adopt an existing instructional model or create its own.

2. **Create lagging indicators for each leading indicator:** Lagging indicators are the evidence that the programs and practices associated with the leading indicators are producing their desired effects. To fulfill this step, a school must first determine what the desired effects of the programs and practices are. Again using leading indicator 2.1 as an example, a school might set a qualitative lagging indicator for the comprehensiveness of the instructional model: "The model provides instructional strategies for a broad array of factors important to teaching such as providing clear goals for academic content, ensuring students feel safe and well-supported, using formative and summative classroom assessments, ensuring that all students are challenged cognitively, and so on." In addition to having a comprehensive schoolwide model of instruction, a school might determine that teachers' awareness of the model is another lagging indicator. For this indicator, the school might establish a quantifiable criterion such as, "At least 90 percent of teachers can describe the school's model of instruction and describe how they use the various parts."

3. **Collect data on the school's status for each lagging indicator:** To fulfill this step, a school must determine the type of data that will indicate whether the programs and practices are having their desired effects at the levels specified by the lagging indicators. For example, relative to the requirement that the schoolwide model of instruction be comprehensive, the school would have to have a written model with the elements spelled out in detail. Additionally, the school might compare their model with at least two other common models of instruction to determine whether their model addresses all important areas of classroom pedagogy. Relative to the lagging indicator that 90 percent of teachers can describe the model and their use of it, the school might create and administer a questionnaire. Leaders wait until programs and practices have had time to exhibit their effects, and then collect data for each lagging indicator.

4. **If the school has not met the minimum requirements for a lagging indicator, refocus attention on the leading indicators by re-examining the programs and practices:** Compare the data collected in step 3 with the minimum requirements in the lagging indicator. If the stated criteria have been met, then this step is complete. If the criteria are not met, then the school re-examines the programs and practices or the type of data collected and makes changes as needed. For example, assume the school compares its instructional model with two other models and notices some areas its model does not cover. The school would then revise its model to add these absent elements. Similarly, if the school notices that the percentage of teachers who can describe the model and how they use it is less than 90 percent, leaders would develop practices to increase the faculty's awareness of the model. When changes have had adequate time to exhibit their effects, collect a second round of data. Repeat this process until the school has met the criteria for a given indicator.

5. **Continue collecting quick data on the effects of the programs and practices for each leading indicator and take appropriate action if problems arise:** By the completion of step 4, a school can consider itself certified for a given level of the HRS model. It is this final step that truly elevates a school to the level of a high reliability organization. Stated differently, once a school has *proven* its performance at a given level, then it must continually collect data on the indicators for that level so that it can identify problems that creep into the system or problems that seem to be on the horizon. This data collection effort does not have to be as intense as the data collection in step 3. In step 5, schools collect *quick data*, or evidence that is pertinent to current performance on specific indicators but is easily collected in a short period of time. For example, for indicator 2.1, in lieu of surveying all teachers in the school, a school administrator might occasionally convene focus groups of teachers to ask them about their understanding of the schools' instructional model and how they are using it in their classrooms.

It is important to note that this five-step process goes well beyond the school effectiveness movement of the 1970s and 1980s as discussed in the introduction (page 1). There, the emphasis was simply on identifying and implementing the programs and practices a school should engage in to be effective. The effectiveness movement at that time did not focus on determining whether those programs and practices were producing their desired effects. To this extent, the HRS process can be considered an extension of the school effectiveness movement of past decades.

Measurement Processes

With the steps for HRS certification in mind, consider the concept of measurement processes. Speaking in more technical terms than we did previously, one might say that a measurement process involves three key components: (1) a description of the underlying construct being measured, (2) a scale to determine status relative to the underlying construct, and (3) rules to assign observations to points on the scale. (For a discussion of rating scales, see *Making Classroom Assessments Reliable and Valid*; Marzano, 2018).

Each of the twenty-five indicators in the HRS framework represents a different underlying construct. Thus, the measurement process is applied to each of the twenty-five elements independently. For example, consider indicator 1.3 in the HRS model: "Teachers have formal roles in the decision-making process regarding school initiatives." This construct lends itself to describing a continuum of actions in which a school might engage—a series of programs and practices, one might say. At one end of the continuum, teachers in a school have absolutely no role in making decisions about school initiatives. At the other end of the continuum, a school employs programs and practices that allow teachers formal input into every decision.

In addition to a description of each construct, a measurement process also has a scale that represents status on the construct and rules for assigning a school a place on the scale. Given the continuum of programs and practices schools might put in place for each element of the HRS framework, we created a scale that describes the extent to which a school is addressing a given leading indicator. The generic form of the scale for all twenty-five elements in the HRS framework appears in figure 1.1. We refer to this type of scale as a *leadership accountability scale* as it is intended to provide guidance to school leaders.

Sustaining (4)	Applying (3)	Developing (2)	Beginning (1)	Not Attempting (0)
The school cultivates information through quick data sources to monitor the leading indicator, *and* it takes proper actions to intervene when quick data indicate a potential problem.	The school has taken specific actions to implement the leading indicator schoolwide, *and* has identified lagging indicators to show the desired effects of these actions.	The school has taken specific actions to implement the leading indicator schoolwide.	The school is in the beginning, yet incomplete, stages of implementing the leading indicator.	The school does not have the leading indicator in place.

Figure 1.1: Generic leadership accountability scale.

At the *not attempting* level (score 0) of the scale, a school has not developed programs and practices to address the indicator in question, nor even attempted to. At this level, the school has not yet taken step 1 of the HRS certification process described in the previous section. This changes at the *beginning* level (score 1) of the scale. At this level, the school attempts to develop programs and practices to address the specific indicator, but the programs and practices are incomplete; there is still work to do to fully address the indicator. It is only when a school reaches the *developing* level (score 2) that it has completed step 1 of the certification process. There the school has indicator-specific programs and practices in place and executes them without significant errors or omissions.

To reach the *applying* level (score 3), a school must prove the effectiveness of its leading indicators with evidence. This requires the execution of steps 2, 3, and 4 in the HRS certification process. Step 2 involves creating lagging indicators. Step 3 requires collecting data relative to the lagging indicators and comparing those data with the criteria for success in the lagging indicator. If the criteria have not been met, then step 4 focuses attention back on the programs and practices for the leading indicators. The school collects new data to compare to the criteria for success.

The highest level of the accountability scale is the *sustaining* level (score 4). Once a school has reached the applying level by gathering data that meet the criterion scores, it adopts a continuous-improvement stance and collects quick data to monitor its programs regularly. This is the essence of the HRS process. When a school reaches this level of operation, it is functioning as a high reliability organization. When a school has reached the sustaining level, it is continuously involved in step 5 of the HRS process.

The five steps of the HRS process require schools to engage in detailed and thoughtful measurement. This noted, any measurement process must be examined in terms of its reliability and its validity. We consider reliability first.

The Reliability of the HRS Measurement Process

Educators commonly use the term *reliability* to refer to how precise a measurement is. While this is an accurate interpretation, when considering the measurement process for HRS, it is necessary to be more technical. A foundational concept in measurement theory is the following equation.

$$\text{Assigned score on a scale} = \text{the true score on the scale} + \text{error score}$$

This equation was formally established in the early 1900s (Thorndike, 1904). In the context of the HRS scales, it means that a school's score for a given indicator consists of two parts: the true score and the error score.

The true score is the part of the assigned score that precisely represents the school's status on the trait measured by the scale. One way of thinking about the true score is that it is the score the school would receive if all information about the school's programs and practices regarding a specific indicator were presented in full detail and judged completely accurately. However, this ideal scenario most probably cannot exist in reality. A school could never actually gather all relevant information regarding an indicator and present it. Even if it could, the individual assigning the score might not interpret the information in a completely accurate manner. Also, the nature of the scale itself introduces error simply because it only has five values. At any point in time for any given indicator, a school might have met all the criteria for one level of the scale as well as some of the criteria for the next level up. Yet a school cannot be assigned the score for the next level up until it meets all criteria for that level. These are all forms of error in the measurement system. Putting aside the technical aspects of the foundational equation articulated above, school leaders can simply keep in mind that any scores they or someone else assigns to their school using the scales in the HRS process will never be pure or completely accurate measures. This awareness should translate into an ongoing attempt to ascertain the most accurate score possible at any moment in time. To this end, a school leader is always interpreting information about the school as new evidence that confirms or brings into question scores currently assigned to the school regarding specific indicators.

Adjustments for the Error Inherent in a Measurement Process

Accounting for measurement error is a foundational aspect of creating an effective measurement system. When it comes to traditional tests designed to measure a person's knowledge or skill, there are a variety of approaches commonly used, including classical test theory (CTT), item-response theory (IRT), and generalizability theory (see Marzano, 2018, for a discussion). CTT uses the foundational equation (assigned score = true score + error score) and can be applied to any situation involving measurement. Ostensibly, we are using CTT to discuss measurement as it relates to HRS. IRT focuses on using the psychometric characteristics of specific test items to generate comprehensive scores. Given its focus on individual tests, it is not a good model to use with the HRS process. As its name implies, generalizability theory focuses on the extent to which data can be generalized beyond the environment in which they were collected. Since the HRS process, by definition, is specific to an individual school, generalizability is not a good model to use with the HRS process. These theories best apply to traditional tests; the error in scales like those used in the HRS process—best generically termed *rating scales*—manifests somewhat differently because they involve judgments made by raters (see Cohen, 1960).

One source of measurement error inherent in rating scales was disclosed in the Measures of Effective Teaching (MET) study regarding how administrators use rating scales to evaluate teachers' pedagogical skills (Bill & Melinda Gates Foundation, 2012). One of the major findings from that study was that administrators tasked with scoring teachers using a specific rating scale didn't actually use the criteria at each level of the scale to assign a score. Instead, raters typically developed their own versions of what the various levels of the scale meant in terms of teacher behavior. More specifically, raters would first form a general impression of a teacher's competence and then assign a score value using their own idiosyncratic criteria. In effect, they ignored the criteria from the original scale.

To avoid this phenomenon with the HRS scales, we developed a protocol that requires raters to consider the criteria at each level of a scale. The protocol is designed to be used as a tool for self-analysis and reflection by school leaders or members of the school engaged in the HRS process. It can also be used by external raters. The protocol is depicted in figure 1.2. Protocols for each indicator appear in the appendix (page 85).

Leading Indicator 1.4: Teacher teams and collaborative groups regularly interact to address common issues regarding curriculum, assessment, instruction, and the achievement of all students.

Step	Score	Begin at step A, Developing, and follow the flow-chart process to determine the status of your school in this leading indicator.	
C	4 Sustaining	The school periodically cultivates data through quick data sources to monitor teacher teams and collaborative groups to meet regularly and address issues regarding curriculum, assessment, instruction, and the achievement of all students, *and* it takes proper actions to intervene when quick data indicate a potential problem.	If yes, Sustaining If no, Applying
B	3 Applying	The school has developed formal, schoolwide processes for teacher teams and collaborative groups to meet regularly and address issues regarding curriculum, assessment, instruction, and the achievement of all students, *and* can provide data and concrete artifacts of practice proving the desired effects of these actions.	If yes, go to step C If no, Developing
A	2 Developing	The school has developed formal, schoolwide processes for teacher teams and collaborative groups to meet regularly and address issues regarding curriculum, assessment, instruction, and the achievement of all students.	If yes, go to step B If no, go to step D
D	1 Beginning	The school is in the beginning, yet incomplete, stages of developing formal processes for teacher teams and collaborative groups to meet regularly and address issues regarding curriculum, assessment, instruction, and the achievement of all students.	If yes, Beginning If no, Not Attempting
	0 Not Attempting	The school has not attempted to develop formal processes for teacher teams and collaborative groups to meet regularly and address issues regarding curriculum, assessment, instruction, and the achievement of all students.	

Figure 1.2: Sample protocol for using leadership accountability scales.

The steps in the protocol are labeled A through D. To analyze the state of this leading indicator, the school leader starts with step A. This first step is at the developing level (score 2) of the scale. In this step, the rater considers the question, "Are we operating at the developing level relative to this particular indicator?" For indicator 1.4, "Teacher teams and collaborative groups regularly interact to address common issues regarding curriculum, assessment, instruction, and the achievement of all students," answering this question requires the school leader to read the description of the developing level for this indicator: "The school has developed formal, schoolwide processes for teacher teams and collaborative groups to meet regularly and address issues regarding curriculum, assessment, instruction, and the achievement of all students." The developing level is the fulcrum of the scale.

Based on the administrator's answer to the question of whether the school is meeting the criteria for the developing level, the leader moves up or down on the scale. If the leader's answer to the question is *no*, the protocol indicates moving to step D, which deals with the beginning level of the scale. Again, the leader reads the criteria at this level: "The school is in the beginning, yet incomplete, stages of developing formal processes for teacher teams and collaborative groups to meet regularly and address issues regarding curriculum, assessment, instruction, and the achievement of all students." The leader then determines whether the school is operating at this level. If the answer is *yes*, then the school receives a score of beginning (1) on this indicator. If the leader's answer is *no*, then the school receives a score of not attempting (0).

Now consider what would happen if the leader made a different determination at the fulcrum of the scale, the developing level (score 2). As indicated by the protocol, if the leader says *yes* to the question of whether the school is operating at the developing level, the leader then moves to step B, which is at the applying level. To rate at this level, the school must meet the following criteria: "The school has developed formal, schoolwide processes for teacher teams and collaborative groups to meet regularly and address issues regarding curriculum, assessment, instruction, and the achievement of all students, *and* can provide data and concrete artifacts of practice proving the desired effects of these actions." If the leader determines the school is *not* functioning at this level, then the school receives a score of developing (2). If the leader determines the school is functioning at this level, then the leader moves to step C, which is at the sustaining level. To be at the sustaining level, the school must meet the following criteria: "The school periodically cultivates data through quick data sources to monitor teacher teams and collaborative groups to meet regularly and address issues regarding curriculum, assessment, instruction, and the achievement of all students, *and* it takes proper actions to intervene when quick data indicate a potential problem." The leader again determines whether the school is functioning at this level. If the answer is *yes*, then the school receives a score of sustaining (4). If the answer is *no*, then the school receives a score of applying (3).

This step-by-step process helps ensure that leaders or other raters consider every level of the scale when determining a school's status on a given indicator. Stated differently, this process helps mitigate the specific type of error highlighted in the MET study regarding rating scales by forcing raters to consider the criteria at all levels of the scale. This goes a long way in increasing the precision of ratings using the HRS scales. To make the scoring process even more precise, the leader can focus on clear criteria for lagging indicators.

Clear Criteria for Lagging Indicators

Another significant source of error when using the HRS scales is not having clear criteria for the beginning, developing, applying, and sustaining levels in each scale. To mitigate this type of error, schools should develop lagging indicators with concrete and quantifiable cut scores. To illustrate, consider figure 1.3, which depicts sample lagging indicators for HRS indicator 1.4. These descriptions might be designed by the school leaders or in a collaborative process involving faculty, staff, and school leaders.

Score	Description of Criteria	Sample Lagging Indicators With Concrete Criteria and Quantifiable Cut Scores
4 Sustaining	The school periodically cultivates data through quick data sources to monitor teacher teams and collaborative groups to meet regularly and address issues regarding curriculum, assessment, instruction, and the achievement of all students, *and* it takes proper actions to intervene when quick data indicate a potential problem.	In addition to the lagging indicator data for the applying level, school leaders regularly collect and analyze quick data like the following: • Drop-in visits to collaborative team meetings are conducted. • Collaborative artifacts, such as copies of common assessments or intervention plans, are collected. • Common assessment data sets are reviewed. • Copies of team agendas or notes from meetings are collected. • Quick discussions with individual teachers regarding the current work of their teams are held. If the data indicate current or potential problems, school leadership develops and executes plans to address those problems.
3 Applying	The school has developed formal, schoolwide processes for teacher teams and collaborative groups to meet regularly and address issues regarding curriculum, assessment, instruction, and the achievement of all students, *and* can provide data and concrete artifacts of practice proving the desired effects of these actions.	Written protocols are in place to guide collaborative teams regarding how teams should operate and what they should produce as a result of their efforts. Additionally, the results of collaborative meetings are documented and regularly collected and analyzed by leaders. At least 90 percent of collaborative teams regularly submit data regarding their results. 100 percent of teachers report that collaborative teams are provided with adequate guidance and feedback.
2 Developing	The school has developed formal, schoolwide processes for teacher teams and collaborative groups to meet regularly and address issues regarding curriculum, assessment, instruction, and the achievement of all students.	Written protocols are in place for the various decisions collaborative teams should make regarding curriculum, instruction, and assessments. Written protocols are in place for the types of outcomes collaborative teams should monitor regarding their decisions. Written protocols are in place regarding how collaborative teams are to report to school leadership.
1 Beginning	The school is in the beginning, yet incomplete, stages of developing formal processes for teacher teams and collaborative groups to meet regularly and address issues regarding curriculum, assessment, instruction, and the achievement of all students.	Some written protocols are in place to guide collaborative teams, or some collaborative teams follow the established protocols, even if those protocols are not complete.
0 Not Attempting	The school has not attempted to develop formal processes for teacher teams and collaborative groups to meet regularly and address issues regarding curriculum, assessment, instruction, and the achievement of all students.	

Figure 1.3: Lagging indicators for HRS indicator 1.4.

Figure 1.3 (page 19) illustrates that clear lagging indicators are more concrete and quantitative articulations of the expected outcomes of the programs and practices identified as the leading indicators. For example, reconsider the general criteria already articulated in the scale for the developing level (score 2): "The school has developed formal, schoolwide processes for teacher teams and collaborative groups to meet regularly and address issues regarding curriculum, assessment, instruction, and the achievement of all students." The sample lagging indicators for the score level depicted in figure 1.3 translate the general intent of the stated criteria in the rating scale into concrete and measurable terms.

- Written protocols are in place for the various decisions collaborative teams should make regarding curriculum, instruction, and assessments.
- Written protocols are in place for the types of outcomes collaborative teams should monitor regarding their decisions.
- Written protocols are in place regarding how collaborative teams are to report to school leadership.

In this case, each criterion at this level requires the school to have written protocols in place.

Following this same trend, note the criteria at the applying level (score 3). Here, some criteria are stated in terms of percentages: at least 90 percent of collaborative teams regularly submit data regarding their results. At the applying level, it is common to state lagging indicators in the form of the percentage of constituents who hold specific perceptions or engage in certain actions. In particular, the first two leading indicators at level 1 of the HRS model reference perceptions of important constituents within the school.

1.1 The faculty and staff perceive the school environment as safe, supportive, and orderly.

1.2 Students, parents, and the community perceive the school environment as safe, supportive, and orderly.

These are the only indicators in the entire HRS framework described in perceptual terms. This is because they both deal with safety, support, and order. Of course, there is an objective reality to safety, support, and order. For example, students must, in fact, be free from physical danger, they must be supported by those around them, and they must have a system of rules and procedures to guide their actions. But even when programs and practices to these ends are in place, some students might not *perceive* they are safe and supported and the environment is orderly. Thus, the evidence that these states do exist in a school must include stakeholder perceptions.

Perceptual Data Within the Measurement Process

As indicated in the preceding discussion, perceptual data can bring clarity to lagging indicators in that leaders can establish a percentage of constituents having specific perceptions as the criterion for a lagging indicator. To this end, there are surveys for each indicator for four audiences: school leader, teachers, students, and parents. But survey data introduce their own unique type of error. To illustrate, reconsider the basic equation from classical test theory we introduced in the initial discussion about error:

Observed score on a survey = the true score on the survey + error score

We have changed the wording of the equation slightly to indicate that we are now discussing scores teachers, administrators, students, and parents give on surveys regarding their perceptions. The interpretation of the equation is still the same. Each person's observed score is made up of two parts: the true score and the error score for that individual. The smaller the error scores across individuals, the more precise the survey. This type of precision is measured by *reliability coefficients*, the values of which range from 1.00, indicating there is no error at all in the measurement, to 0.00, indicating that the measurement is entirely error. Neither of these extremes is ever found in educational measurements. Figure 1.4 presents reliability coefficients for the level 1 HRS surveys.

	Item Count	α	n
1.1: The faculty and staff perceive the school environment as safe and orderly.	6	0.82	417
1.2: Students, parents, and the community perceive the school environment as safe and orderly.	7	0.80	246
1.3: Teachers have formal roles in the decision-making process regarding school initiatives.	5	0.88	333
1.4: Teacher teams and collaborative groups regularly interact to address common issues regarding curriculum, assessment, instruction, and the achievement of all students.	7	0.85	321
1.5: Teachers and staff have formal ways to provide input regarding the optimal functioning of the school.	4	0.86	298
1.6: Students, parents, and the community have formal ways to provide input regarding the optimal functioning of the school.	9	0.89	167
1.7: The success of the whole school, as well as individuals within the school, is appropriately acknowledged.	5	0.92	405
1.8: The fiscal, operational, and technological resources of the school are managed in a way that directly supports teachers.	7	0.90	254
All survey items	50	0.97	113

Source: © 2015 by Marzano Resources. Used with permission.

Figure 1.4: Coefficient alpha reliabilities for HRS level 1 surveys.

Figure 1.4 depicts the results of a reliability study (Haystead, 2015) conducted on the survey scores of 457 respondents collected in May 2013. Analysts calculated a type of reliability coefficient called *Cronbach's* α (alpha) for each indicator at level 1 of the HRS framework. Cronbach's α is a measure of the internal consistency of a scale (such as a summated rating scale with six items). A widely accepted rule of thumb suggests that Cronbach's α should be at least 0.70 for a scale to demonstrate internal consistency (Spector, 1992). As shown in figure 1.4, the reliabilities for the eight indicators at level 1 range from 0.80 to 0.92. The reliability of the aggregate score across the eight categories was 0.97. All reliability coefficients were well above the 0.70 threshold. (For a detailed discussion of this study, see Haystead, 2015). The main conclusion leaders can take away from the findings in figure 1.4 is that perceptual data from the HRS surveys represent a reliable form of information they can use when establishing lagging indicators.

Layers of Reviews and Reviewers

The final way the HRS process attempts to account for measurement error is to employ an iterative process to arrive at a final score for each indicator at each level. Stated differently, schools do not simply submit all of their evidence at a given point in time for a given indicator and then receive a summative score for that indicator. Rather, when evidence is submitted, it is reviewed by a Marzano Resources rater in a timely fashion. If that evidence (expressed as lagging indicators) does not demonstrate that the school is operating at an appropriate level of effectiveness in terms of the expected outcomes for that indicator or has not made sufficient increases in the expected outcomes for that indicator, then the school must establish new lagging indicators and submit more data at a later point in time.

To illustrate, consider indicator 2.1: "The school communicates a clear vision as to how teachers should address instruction." Assume that one of the lagging indicators the school establishes for this element is that the model of instruction addresses the basic categories of at least two other well-known instructional models. Also assume that the school does, indeed, formally compare its instructional model with others. The Marzano Resources rater, however, might note that the two models the school selected for comparison are fairly narrow in scope themselves and ask the school to add one other model known for its comprehensiveness to the comparison process. The school complies and adds the recommended model to the comparison process. As a result, the school adds some components to its instructional model to make it more comprehensive. In effect, this protocol helps address error at the individual element level, in an iterative manner. In this case, the error the school has fallen into is to set a criterion for a lagging indicator that is not sufficient. In a manner of speaking, the criterion in the lagging indicator is too low. When a rater detects error, it is communicated to the school, which then has the invitation and opportunity to rectify the error.

Finally, after a school has submitted evidence for certification and the school's rater has accepted the evidence, a second rater who did not interact with the school reviews the school's evidence. This adds a second layer of scrutiny to each certification. The second-level reviewer examines the evidence the school submitted for every indicator to make sure that criteria for lagging indicators are sufficiently rigorous and that the school has provided sufficient evidence that it has met the criteria. If the second-level reviewer has a question about either of these aspects of the certification process, they report the issue back to the first-level reviewer, who seeks further information to reconcile the issue. The second-level reviewer is also responsible for keeping track of individual reviewers' tendencies to ensure that all reviewers hold schools to the same standards. When a reviewer appears to be using standards different from those that other reviewers have been trained to use, the first-level reviewer is required to go through additional training and demonstrate recognition of the discrepancies and correction thereof.

The Validity of the HRS Measurement Process

Validity is another characteristic one must consider when analyzing the efficacy of a measurement process. As is the case with the term *reliability*, most educators have a general understanding of validity. They typically interpret validity as the extent to which an assessment measures what it purports to measure. As is the case with reliability, there is much more to validity than this general understanding.

To be sure, the initial conception of validity was consistent with the general understanding educators have today. As Henry Garrett noted in 1937, "the fidelity with which [a test] measures what it purports to measure" (p. 324) is the hallmark of its validity. By the 1950s, though, the concept of validity had become much more robust and nuanced. As explained by Samuel Messick (1993), since the early 1950s, validity has been thought of as involving three major types: criterion-related validity, construct validity, and content validity. In addition to the three types of validity, there are two perspectives from which one can consider a measurement process: the instrumental perspective and the argument-based perspective (Hathcoat, 2013). Validity in general and the three different types in particular look quite different depending on which perspective one takes. We explain instrumental and argument-based perspectives on each of the three types as they relate to rating scales in the following sections.

The Instrumental Perspective of Validity

The instrumental perspective focuses on the measurement tool itself. When the tool is a traditional test, validity involves the extent to which the test actually measures students' knowledge of important content for the topic the test purports to measure. If a test is designed to measure fifth-grade mathematics content, then the validity of the test would be a function of the extent to which the test actually has items that deal with the important fifth-grade mathematics information and skills. According to John Hathcoat (2013), this has been the traditional perspective in measurement theory regarding a specific test.

All three types of validity can be defined from the instrumental perspective. To establish criterion-related validity for a traditional test from the instrumental perspective, the newly developed test is mathematically compared to some other assessment already considered a valid measure of the topic. For example, to determine the criterion validity for a newly developed test of fifth-grade mathematics, the test designers would have to find an existing test that is already accepted as a valid measure of fifth-grade mathematics. This second assessment is referred to as the *criterion measure*, hence the term *criterion-related validity*. A correlation coefficient is then computed between the new test and the criterion measure. A test is considered valid for any criterion with which it has a high correlation (Guilford, 1946).

The major issue with criterion-related validity when it comes to rating scales is that it is difficult in many cases to identify an appropriate criterion measure for the construct that is being rated. Citing the work of Roderick Chisholm (1973), Hathcoat (2013) exemplified the criterion problem using the example of quality of apples:

> If we wish to identify apple quality then we need a criterion to distinguish "good" apples from "bad" apples. We may choose to sort apples into different piles based upon color though any criterion is adequate for this example. The problem arises whenever we ask whether our criterion worked in that color actually separated good apples from bad apples. How can we investigate our criterion without already knowing something about which apples are good and bad? (pp. 2–3)

Construct validity became prominent about halfway through the 20th century. According to Hathcoat (2013), a seminal article in 1955 by Lee Cronbach and Paul Meehl led to a focus on construct validity. Hathcoat explained that Cronbach and Meehl were concerned about situations for which a target domain or a relevant criterion was ambiguous. To a certain extent, Cronbach and Meehl were recommending that construct validity applies to any type of content for which it is difficult to find criterion measures. For example, where it is rather easy to find a criterion measure for fifth-grade mathematics, it is quite difficult to find criterion measures for content like students' abilities to apply knowledge in unique situations or students' abilities to make good decisions.

Construct validity is typically determined by performing a statistical procedure referred to as *factor analysis*. Briefly, factor analysis is a process that mathematically provides evidence regarding the extent to which items on a test measure the same construct—hence the term *construct validity*. This is accomplished by computing the correlations between each item on a test with every other item. This intercorrelation matrix is then analyzed mathematically to determine whether there are any items not correlated with the others on the test. If all items are correlated with the other items, then the test is determined to possess construct validity. This procedure is not amenable to rating scales like those used in the HRS process simply because it requires the presence of multiple items answered by multiple people.

Finally, content validity reaffirms the general definition of validity as held by most educators. A test has content validity if it contains items that appear to measure the important information relative to the target content. An assessment of fifth-grade mathematics would be considered as having content validity, for example, if a panel of experts on mathematics curriculum at the fifth-grade level examined the items on the test and concluded that those items addressed the content important for fifth graders to know. A rating scale for a particular HRS indicator would be considered as having content validity if it explicitly addresses the important programs and practices for the construct it is designed to measure.

In summary, from the instrumental perspective, a rating scale like those used in the HRS process addresses only one of three common types of validity: content validity. However, from the argument-based perspective, the HRS rating scales have a much stronger connection to the various types of validity.

The Argument-Based Perspective of Validity

The argument-based perspective of validity can be traced back to work in the 1970s and 1980s around the importance of test interpretation (Messick, 1975, 1993), but it is relatively new in its wide use among educational researchers, which is largely due to a series of works by Michael Kane (1992, 2001, 2009). At its core, argument-based validity involves an interpretive argument that "lays the network of inferences leading from the test scores [or rating scale scores] to the conclusions to be drawn and any decisions to be based on these conclusions" (Kane, 2001, p. 329).

From the instrumental perspective, it is the assessment itself or the rating scale itself that possesses a specific type of validity (criterion, construct, or content). In contrast, from the argument-based perspective, validity is a function of how scorers use the data generated from the assessment or rating scale to craft an argument regarding a score for a particular student's knowledge or skill or a score for a particular school's status on an HRS indicator. This necessarily changes how the three types of validity are viewed.

From the argument-based perspective, criterion-related validity for a rating is a function of how well the HRS rating predicts the school's performance on the lagging indicators (that is, the criteria) for the particular element being rated. For example, if a school is rated at the developing (2) level for indicator 1.4 ("The school has developed formal, schoolwide processes for teacher teams and collaborative groups to meet regularly and address issues regarding curriculum, assessment, instruction, and the achievement of all students"), then, by definition, the school would have one or more lagging indicators that specify how collaborative teams should interact to ensure that team members are following the same unit designs for a specific topic. The school would also have one or more lagging indicators that specify how to create and interpret common assessments on the topics addressed in the unit. Finally, the school would have one or more lagging indicators that specify which instructional strategies it should use during the units of instruction.

From the argument-based perspective, construct validity for a given rating scale is determined by the extent to which those administering the scale and those being measured by the scale are clear about the progression of actions that signify different levels on the rating scale. For example, the rating scale for HRS indicator 1.4 would be judged as having construct validity if the raters using the scale to measure a school and the leaders in the school being measured all have a clear understanding of the specific types of programs and practices that would move them from the developing level to the applying level.

From the argument-based perspective, content validity for a given HRS rating scale is determined by the extent to which the rating scale provides school leaders and staff with clear guidance in adopting, adapting, or developing programs and practices that produce the desired outcome for the lagging indicators. This validity characteristic is directly addressed by the fact that HRS scales require schools to specify both leading and lagging indicators for their school. Again, consider figure 1.3 (page 19). At the developing level, school leaders have specified that written protocols must be in place for the actions of collaborative teams relative to how they interact about the issues of curriculum, assessment, and instruction. At the applying level, school leaders have specified the percentages of teachers who must respond in specific ways and engage in specific actions. This type of guidance is actionable in concrete ways.

These characteristics of the argument-based perspective as they relate to HRS rating scales are summarized in table 1.1.

Table 1.1: Three Types of Argument-Based Validity When Using a Rating Scale

Validity Type	Argument-Based Perspective for HRS Rating Scales
Criterion-Related Validity	The extent to which a school's HRS rating predicts the school's performance on the lagging indicators for the particular element being rated.
Construct Validity	The extent to which those administering the scale and those being measured by the scale are clear about the progression of actions that signify different levels on the rating scale.
Content Validity	The extent to which the rating scale provides school leaders and staff with clear guidance in adopting, adapting, or developing programs and practices that produce the desired outcome relative to the lagging indicators.

In effect, the traditional, instrumental view of the three types of validity does not mesh well with rating scales like those used in the HRS certification process. However, when viewed from the argument-based perspective, such scales are strong measurement tools.

HRS in Practice

Many, if not most, schools initially approach the HRS process as an intervention, a set of programs and practices that they must implement. The realization that it is a measurement process usually becomes apparent when school leaders and their teachers and staff must identify lagging indicators for the programs and practices they already had in place for some time or have recently put in place. While there is always a rater guiding their deliberations, schools must identify the type of data they will collect as lagging indicators and criterion scores they must reach on their lagging indicators. The seminal point here is that schools do this not for some external audience, but for themselves and their own sense of institutional agency. This allows school leaders great flexibility in identifying the metrics that are most useful to them.

This flexibility is particularly apparent with HRS indicator 3.4: "The school establishes clear and measurable goals that are focused on critical needs regarding improving overall student achievement at the school level." While many schools use their end-of-year scores on state tests to set lagging indicator criteria, a significant proportion use other metrics they feel are the most accurate measures of students' learning in their school to set goals for student achievement. For example, one principal at an alternative secondary school commonly had students for a relatively short period of time and felt the end-of-year test wasn't sensitive enough to the knowledge gain of students who had only been at the school for only a few months. Consequently, the principal, in conjunction with school faculty, developed the metric of units passed on a specific self-paced online program within a grading period. Another principal at an elementary school selected scores from interim assessments as the criterion scores for student achievement in reading but used the end-of-year state test scores for student achievement in mathematics. The freedom to use criteria that are most meaningful to the school also shows up prominently in HRS indicator 1.1: "The faculty and staff perceive the school environment as safe, supportive, and orderly." Many schools use the data generated from school behavioral management programs that provide detailed reports on such behaviors as disruptions in the classroom, disruptions in the hallways, incidents of bullying, and the like as the criterion scores for this indicator.

An interesting phenomenon with some leaders in HRS schools is they come to view the measurement process within HRS as a useful internal management tool. To illustrate, one elementary principal who was seeking HRS level 1 certification was in her first year as a principal when she started the certification process. She reported that the certification process became a road map for her as to what she should be working on and how to select or create programs and practices that met specific needs in her school. She particularly appreciated the concept of lagging indicators with concrete criteria established by her and her team. The measurement process became a dynamic set of guidelines and ways of collecting data with which to make informed decisions for the betterment of the school.

Another, more seasoned middle school principal likened the HRS process to getting and staying in shape. She was a runner herself and would periodically train for various races. She would use the forthcoming race as the impetus to ensure that all aspects of her life were working in concert for her to operate at her peak physically. This was the way in which she viewed HRS certification both in terms of the process itself and the results it produces. She also used this metaphor with her faculty and staff. Certification was an opportunity for them to operate at higher levels and generate the proof that they were at those levels.

Insights and Actions

The most salient insight relative to this big idea is that the HRS process is not a program or practice to be implemented and then forgotten. Rather, the programs and practices that are part of every level are choices individual schools must make. Another insight is that the measurement process never ends. Even when schools have been certified at a given level, they continue to monitor the effectiveness of programs and practices in their school. The most salient action that stems from this big idea is that schools search for or create efficient measurement tools to gauge their current levels of effectiveness for various indicators.

Big Idea 2

Certain Levels of the HRS Framework Have a More Direct Relationship to Student Achievement as Measured by External Tests Than Others

It's probably safe to say that the success of most schools in the United States is judged primarily by the scores their students receive on some type of external test. Most states administer specific tests for the purpose of determining the success of individual schools and the students within those schools. This has been both an implicit and explicit expectation of K–12 schools in the United States since the Elementary and Secondary Education Act of 1965 and its reauthorization in 2015 (U.S. Government, 2022). Table 2.1 (page 28) depicts the various external tests used in the fifty states and District of Columbia.

There is an intuitive logic to using external tests of student learning as the primary criterion for determining the effectiveness of a school. If one of the main functions of schools is to ensure that students learn important academic content, then state governments must have a way to ensure that students in their schools are, in fact, learning that content. To ensure that measures of student learning are comparable across the entire state, the department of education in each state should design and administer common assessments for the major topics that are explicit in the state's standards. This line of reasoning appears to represent a very straightforward set of goals and ways to determine whether those goals have been met. However, when one examines the actual practice of testing across the United States, this seemingly effective and efficient system unravels rather quickly.

The Truth About Performance on External Tests

There is a set of assumptions that underlies the interpretation of test scores and how educators use them to make decisions about individual students. Those assumptions are as follows.

- An external test assesses all the important content in a given subject area.
- An external test is the most accurate way to measure an individual student's knowledge of a subject area.

We consider each of these assumptions in the following sections.

Table 2.1: External Tests by State

State	Administrating Agency	Test Name
Alabama	Alabama State Department of Education	ACT
Alaska	Alaska Department of Education and Early Development	Alaska Measures of Progress
Arizona	Arizona Department of Education	ACT and ACT Aspire Arizona's Academic Standards Assessment AzSCI (Arizona's Science Test)
Arkansas	Arkansas Department of Education	ACT Arkansas Teaching and Learning Assessment System National Assessment of Educational Progress (NAEP)
California	California Department of Education	California Assessment of Student Performance and Progress
Colorado	Colorado Department of Education	Colorado Measures of Academic Success
Connecticut	Connecticut State Department of Education	Connecticut Academic Performance Test Smarter Balanced Assessment
Delaware	Delaware Department of Education	Delaware System of Student Assessment
District of Columbia	District of Columbia Public Schools	Partnership for Assessment of Readiness for College and Careers
Florida	Florida Department of Education	Florida Standards Assessments Florida Standards Alternate Assessment

Georgia	Georgia Department of Education	Georgia Milestones:
		  • End-of-Course Test (grades 9–12)
		  • End-of-Grade Test (grades 3–8)
		Georgia Alternate Assessment

Hawaii	Hawaii State Department of Education	Hawaii State Assessment Hawaii State Alternative Assessment
Idaho	Idaho State Department of Education	Idaho Standards Achievement Test
Illinois	Illinois State Board of Education	Illinois Assessment of Readiness Illinois Science Assessment
Indiana	Indiana Department of Education	Indiana Learning Evaluation and Assessment Readiness Network
Iowa	Iowa Department of Education	Iowa Statewide Assessment of Student Progress Iowa Tests of Educational Development
Kansas	Kansas State Department of Education	Kansas History, Government, Economics and Geography Assessment Kansas Mathematics Assessment Kansas Reading Assessment Kansas Science Assessment Kansas Writing Assessment
Kentucky	Kentucky Department of Education	Kentucky Summative Assessment
Louisiana	Louisiana Department of Education	Louisiana Educational Assessment Program (LEAP) Integrated LEAP
Maine	Maine Department of Education	Maine Comprehensive Assessment System Maine Educational Assessments
Maryland	Maryland State Department of Education	Maryland Comprehensive Assessment Program
Massachusetts	Massachusetts Department of Elementary and Secondary Education	Massachusetts Comprehensive Assessment System
Michigan	Michigan Department of Education	Michigan Student Test of Educational Progress
Minnesota	Minnesota Department of Education	Minnesota Comprehensive Assessments—Series II
Mississippi	Mississippi Department of Education	ACT English Language Proficiency Test Mississippi Academic Assessment Program NAEP
Missouri	Missouri Department of Elementary and Secondary Education	Missouri Assessment Program
Montana	Montana Office of Public Instruction	ACT Montana Science Assessment Smarter Balanced Assessment

Nebraska	Nebraska Department of Education	ACT NAEP Nebraska Student-Centered Assessment System
Nevada	Nevada Department of Education	Nevada State Assessment System
New Hampshire	New Hampshire Department of Education	New Hampshire Statewide Assessment System
New Jersey	New Jersey Department of Education	New Jersey Student Learning Assessments
New Mexico	New Mexico Public Education Department	New Mexico Alternate Performance Assessment New Mexico Measures of Student Success and Achievement
New York	New York State Education Department	Regents Examinations
North Carolina	North Carolina Department of Public Instruction	North Carolina End-of-Grade Tests (grades 3–8) North Carolina End-of-Course Tests (grades 9–12)
North Dakota	North Dakota Department of Public Instruction	North Dakota State Assessment
Ohio	Ohio Department of Education	Ohio's State Tests
Oklahoma	Oklahoma State Department of Education	Oklahoma School Testing Program
Oregon	Oregon Department of Education	Oregon Statewide Assessment System
Pennsylvania	Pennsylvania Department of Education	Keystone Exams Pennsylvania Alternate System of Assessment Pennsylvania System of School Assessment
Rhode Island	Rhode Island Department of Education	Rhode Island Comprehensive Assessment System
South Carolina	South Carolina Department of Education	End-of-Course Examination Program South Carolina College- and Career-Ready Assessments South Carolina Palmetto Assessment of State Standards
South Dakota	South Dakota Department of Education	South Dakota Assessment System
Tennessee	Tennessee Department of Education	Tennessee Comprehensive Assessment Program
Texas	Texas Education Agency	State of Texas Assessments of Academic Readiness
Utah	Utah State Board of Education	RISE Utah Aspire Plus
Vermont	Vermont Agency of Education	Vermont Comprehensive Assessment System
Virginia	Virginia Department of Education	Standards of Learning
Washington	Washington Office of Superintendent of Public Instruction	Smarter Balanced Assessment Washington Comprehensive Assessment of Science
West Virginia	West Virginia Department of Education	West Virginia General Summative Assessment
Wisconsin	Wisconsin Department of Public Instruction	Wisconsin Forward Exam
Wyoming	Wyoming Department of Education	Wyoming Test of Proficiency and Progress

Source: Alabama State Department of Education, n.d.; Alaska Department of Education and Early Development, n.d.; Arizona Department of Education, n.d.; Arkansas Department of Education, 2023; California Department of Education, 2022, 2023; Colorado Department of Education, n.d.; Connecticut State Department of Education, n.d.; Delaware Department of Education, n.d.; Florida Department of Education, n.d.a, n.d.b; Georgia Department of Education, n.d.a, n.d.b, n.d.c, n.d.d, n.d.e; Hawaii State Department of Education, n.d.; Idaho State Department of Education, n.d.; Illinois State Board of Education, n.d.; Indiana Department of Education, n.d.; Iowa Department of Education, n.d.; Kansas State Department of Education, n.d.; Kentucky Department of Education, 2023; Louisiana Department of Education, n.d.; Maine Department of Education, n.d.; Maryland State Department of Education, n.d.; Massachusetts Department of Elementary and Secondary Education, 2023; Michigan Department of Education, n.d.; Minnesota Department of Education, n.d.; Mississippi Department of Education, n.d.; Missouri Department of Elementary and Secondary Education, n.d.; Montana Office of Public Instruction, n.d.; Nebraska Department of Education, 2023; Nevada Department of Education, n.d.; New Hampshire Department of Education, n.d.; New Jersey Department of Education, n.d.; New Mexico Public Education Department, 2023; New York State Education Department, n.d.a, n.d.b; North Carolina Department of Public Instruction, n.d.; North Dakota Department of Public Instruction, n.d.; Office of the State Superintendent of Education, n.d.; Ohio Department of Education, n.d.; Oklahoma State Department of Education, 2023; Oregon Department of Education, n.d.; Pennsylvania Department of Education, n.d.; Rhode Island Department of Education, n.d.a, n.d.b; South Carolina Department of Education, n.d.; South Dakota Department of Education, n.d.; Tennessee Department of Education, n.d.; Texas Education Agency, n.d.; Utah State Board of Education, n.d.; Vermont Agency of Education, n.d.; Virginia Department of Education, n.d.; Washington Office of Superintendent of Public Instruction, n.d.; West Virginia Department of Education, n.d.; Wisconsin Department of Public Instruction, n.d.; Wyoming Department of Education, n.d.

An External Test Assesses All the Important Content in a Given Subject Area

The source of the content addressed in a state test designed by an external testing company is usually the state's standards documents. This seems like a perfect situation for test design. States have their standards documents. Testing companies simply consult these documents when designing tests for a particular state. Unfortunately, this perceived situation is not reality. This becomes apparent when one examines state standards documents.

State standards documents, although good at providing general goals for curriculum, instruction, and assessment within a state, simply are not conducive to direct translation into reliable and valid tests. In fact, they inherently contain many obstacles to effective test construction. The problems with state standards documents are addressed in depth in the book *The New Art and Science of Classroom Assessment* (Marzano, Norford, & Ruyle, 2019). Here we address these problems briefly. Robert J. Marzano, Jennifer S. Norford, and Mike Ruyle (2019) assert that there are at least three reasons why standards do not provide adequate guidance in designing assessments: (1) too much content, (2) redundancy in standards, and (3) equivocal standard statements. The following sections expound on each of these problems before discussing their impacts on assessments.

Too Much Content

To illustrate the problem of too much content, consider the following middle school mathematics standard, which is an example of a typical articulation of content: "Understands the properties of operations with rational numbers (e.g., distributive property, commutative and associative properties of addition and multiplication, inverse properties, identity properties)" (Mid-Continent Research for Education and Learning, 2014). Marzano and colleagues (2019) noted that decomposing or "unpacking" this standard reveals at least five topics:

1. Understanding the distributive property with rational numbers
2. Understanding the commutative and associative properties of addition with rational numbers
3. Understanding the commutative and associative properties of multiplication with rational numbers
4. Understanding the inverse properties of rational numbers
5. Understanding the identity properties of rational numbers

The problem demonstrated by this mathematics standard exists in virtually every subject area. Robert J. Marzano, David C. Yanoski, Jan K. Hoegh, and Julia A. Simms (2013) explained that standards documents typically pack multiple topics and content into a single statement. To illustrate, they identified seventy-three standards statements for eighth-grade English language arts (ELA) within the Common Core State Standards (National Governors Association Center for Best Practices & Council of Chief State School Officers [CCSSO], 2010a, 2010b, 2010c, n.d.a, n.d.b). An average of five topics embedded in each standard statement expands an eighth-grade ELA teacher's responsibility to 365 topics in a single 180-day school year. While many states have created their own versions of standards for various subject areas, this problem remains and will continue as long as states continue to follow the convention of listing multiple types of knowledge and skill in a single standards statement. We assert that even a cursory examination of state standards indicates that this practice is still very common.

Redundancy in Standards

Redundancy in standards occurs when multiple standards include the same knowledge or skill stated in different ways. In her analysis of the standards as stated in the Common Core, Julia A. Simms (2016) found that they include a great amount of redundant content. As one example, Simms identified overlapping content in six different standards or benchmark statements. This is depicted in figure 2.1.

Unpacked Component Part	Standard
Assess whether the evidence is relevant in an argument	RI.8.8
Assess whether the evidence is sufficient in an argument	
Assess whether the evidence is relevant in a specific claim	
Assess whether the evidence is sufficient in a specific claim	
Recognize when irrelevant evidence is introduced	
Support claims with logical reasoning	W.8.1b
Support claims with relevant evidence	
Acknowledge the claim from alternative claims	W.8.1a
Acknowledge the claim from opposing claims	
Distinguish the claim from alternate claims	
Distinguish the claim from opposing claims	
Write arguments to support claims with clear reasons	W.8.1
Write arguments to support claims with relevant evidence	
Evaluate the relevance of the evidence for a speaker's arguments	
Evaluate the sufficiency of the evidence for a speaker's argument	SL.8.3
Identify when relevant evidence is introduced in a speaker's argument	
Evaluate the relevance of the evidence in a speaker's specific claims	
Evaluate the sufficiency of the evidence for a speaker's specific claims	
Identify when irrelevant evidence is introduced in a speaker's specific claims	
Acknowledge new information expressed by others	SL.8.1d
When warranted, justify their own views in light of the evidence	
When warranted, qualify their own views in light of the evidence presented by others	

Source for standards: NGA & CCSSO, 2010a.
Source: Marzano et al., 2019, pp. 14–15.

Figure 2.1: Overlapping components in ELA standards at the eighth grade.

Figure 2.1 depicts twenty-two statements regarding what students should know and be able to do embedded in six standards. These all deal with claims, evidence, and reasoning even though they use different phrasing. For example, "Support claims with relevant evidence" (W.8.1b) and "Write arguments to support claims with relevant evidence" (W.8.1) restate the same skill of using appropriate evidence to support written claims. Similarly, the reading standard "Recognize when irrelevant evidence is introduced" (RI.8.8) and the speaking and listening standard "Identify when irrelevant evidence is introduced in a speaker's specific claims" (SL.8.3) essentially speak to the same skill, though in different domains. As with the issue of too much content, the problem of redundancy occurs frequently across state standards documents, particularly with knowledge and skills involving reasoning, such as argumentation, problem solving, decision making, and the like.

Equivocal Standard Statements

The problem of equivocal standards is closely related to the problem of too much content. In fact, one might think of the problem of equivocal standards as a subset of the problem of too much content. Too much content occurs when a standard explicitly or implicitly addresses so much content that it would be difficult for a teacher to translate it into a specific lesson. The previous example for too much content includes five different properties across all rational numbers with some of the properties focused specifically on addition and multiplication. Certainly, these are related, but the total amount of content is so vast as to be problematic or impossible for a teacher to address. Equivocal standards can be more focused but still present teachers with problems in terms of what they are expected to teach and assess. To illustrate, consider the following statement from the 2023 Indiana Academic Standards at the fifth-grade level:

> Solve real-world problems involving addition and subtraction of fractions referring to the same whole, including cases of unlike denominators (e.g., by using visual fraction models and equations to represent the problem). Use benchmark fractions and number sense of fractions to estimate mentally and assess whether the answer is reasonable. (Indiana Department of Education, 2023)

The first sentence of this standard is focused and direct and should be rather easy for fifth-grade teachers to translate into a set of lessons. The second statement adds a related but different skill: the ability to estimate mentally and judge the reasonableness of an answer. While this is certainly a useful skill, it is unlike the knowledge and skills articulated in the first sentence, leaving the teacher with questions like how to score students if they can demonstrate proficiency on the first part of the standard but not the second part.

Practical Impacts on Assessments

In summary, standards documents are not great resources if one wishes to create clearly focused assessments of students' academic knowledge and skill. Because of the large amount of content, ambiguity, and redundancy in those state standards documents, test makers have no choice but to sample content and then build items around those samples.

Sampling presents its own series of issues in that it has myriad technical consequences in terms of the comparability of students' scores from one test to another (Berman, Haertel, & Pellegrino, 2020; DePascale & Gong, 2020; Keng & Marion, 2020). Stated differently, sampling makes it almost impossible to ensure that a given test includes the important topics in a given content area or that the items themselves are true representations of what students are learning in class. This sets up a hit-or-miss phenomenon for schools. The teachers in a school might do a good job of teaching specific content embedded in their state standards, but if that content is not what appears on the external test, their students might do poorly in the test even though they have learned the content that was directly taught to them.

Probably the most important awareness educators should cultivate as a result of the inherent limitations of standards documents as the basis for external tests is that the traditional view of the relationship between what is taught, what is learned, and what is tested simply doesn't apply well. Educators in general and curriculum specialists in particular have implicitly or explicitly used the model in figure 2.2 to describe the relationship between three types of curricula: the intended curriculum, the taught curriculum, and the assessed curriculum.

The intended curriculum represents the knowledge and skills every student should know and be able to do for specific subject areas, grade levels, and courses. Of course, this curriculum is typically articulated in the state standards documents. This ideally forms the basis for what is explicitly taught in classrooms (that is, the taught curriculum); what is taught ideally forms the basis for what is tested (that is, the assessed curriculum).

From the preceding discussions about state standards, it is clear that the ideal relationship between the three curricula depicted in figure 2.2 is impossible within the current reality of existing standards documents and external tests. Given the volume, redundancy, and equivocal nature of standards documents, it is difficult if not impossible to obtain a clear accounting of the intended curriculum. Even if a school could completely articulate the implicit and explicit content in the standards documents (that is, the intended curriculum), the school could not teach it all due to the number of standards and amount of content therein. Finally, even if the taught curriculum could completely address the intended curriculum, the assessed curriculum vis-à-vis an external test might emphasize knowledge and skill not emphasized in the taught curriculum.

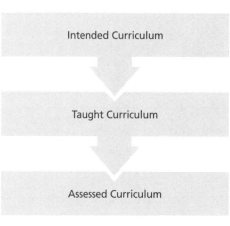

Source: © 2021 by Robert J. Marzano.

Figure 2.2: Ideal relationship between the three curricula.

To make matters worse, a 2022 study has disclosed another impediment to the efficacy of external tests. In the book *Ethical Test Preparation in the Classroom*, Robert J. Marzano, Christopher W. Dodson, Julia A. Simms, and Jacob P. Wipf (2022) analyzed over 8,800 items from state, national, and international tests in mathematics, English language arts, and science. One of their findings was that the items on the tests themselves included a type of thinking that was not a formal part of the subject matter content the items were designed to test. To illustrate, consider the fourth-grade reading item in figure 2.3. Prior to answering this item, students are instructed to read a passage that has been provided to them.

Part A	**Part B**
Which sentence best states a theme in the story?	Which detail from the story best shows this theme?
a. We all have different strengths.	a. "Ah! But quantity is not quality, and your skin is not nearly so tough as mine. . . ." (Paragraph 3)
b. We should try to be patient with others.	b. "The Crocodile, being used to the water, reached the opposite banks of the river first. . . ." (Paragraph 10)
c. We all have the power to help others.	c. " . . . a sudden lurch caused the prize to slip off and sink to the bottom." (Paragraph 12)
d. We should always put forth our best effort.	d. "You are both wise and clever in your respective ways." (Paragraph 13)

Source: © 2021 by Marzano Academies. Adapted with permission.

Figure 2.3: Fourth-grade reading item designed to assess reading comprehension.

On the surface, this item seems straightforward. Students simply read a passage and then identify its main idea or theme. However, as described in *Ethical Test Preparation in the Classroom* (Marzano et al., 2022), main idea and theme are frequently defined differently from item to item. To illustrate, figure 2.4 depicts the various text characteristics that commonly communicate the main idea or theme for fourth-grade reading material.

The main idea or theme is the overarching structure or frame of the passage. A passage can have smaller structures or frames embedded in the overarching structure. The various types of structures that might contain the main idea or theme of a passage include:

- Basic cause and effect (for example, observing that Charlie in *Charlie and the Chocolate Factory* wins the contest because all the other children behave badly)
- Simple chronologies (for example, recalling the order and cause of each child's exit in the story *Charlie and the Chocolate Factory*)
- Problems with simple solutions (for example, observing that the problem of poverty within Charlie's family is solved only by having more money)
- Plots with single storylines (for example, observing that the plot in *Charlie and the Chocolate Factory* involves Charlie's ability to save both his poor family and a lonely man and the storyline follows the boy's strange journey through the factory)

Source: © 2021 by Marzano Academies. Adapted with permission.

Figure 2.4: Fourth-grade text structures that communicate main idea or theme.

Students must also have a general awareness of how they should navigate items like this. Consequently, teachers should provide students with strategies like those in figure 2.5.

When trying to determine the main idea or theme of a passage, your first job is to determine the overall structure of the information in the text. You should consider four types of possible structures: basic cause and effect, simple chronologies, simple problem-solution structure, and stories with one main storyline.

Basic cause and effect:

- Texts that have a cause-and-effect structure contain clues as to what the main idea or theme is. These clues include:
  - Certain words and phrases are commonly used: cause, because, due to, result, sequence, consequence.
  - Look for headings, subheadings, or other text features that indicate cause and effect. For example, data displays might contain information about cause and effect.
- Try to recognize the clues about this structure and mark sections of the text that have them.
- When you are finished reading, try to describe a central causal relationship in a few sentences.

Simple chronologies:

- Texts that have a simple chronology structure contain clues as to what the main idea or theme is. These clues include:
  - Certain words and phrases are commonly used: first, second, next, last, before, after.
  - Look for headings, subheadings, or other textual clues that indicate a sequence of events. For example, chapter titles might provide a clue about the events that happen in the chapter.
- Try to recognize the clues about this structure and mark sections of the text that have them.
- When you are finished reading, try to describe the major events or steps in a sequence or chronology in a few sentences.

Simple problem-solution structure:

- Texts that have a problem-solution structure contain clues as to what the main idea or theme is. These clues include:
  - Certain words and phrases are commonly used: issue, problem, cause, challenge, obstacle, strategy, solve, solution, resolution, fix.
  - Headings and subheadings often indicate the presentation of a problem followed by discussion of one or more solutions.

- Try to recognize the clues about this structure and mark sections of the text that have them.
- When you are finished reading, try to describe the problem and its solution in a few sentences.

Story with one main storyline:

- Texts that have one main storyline contain clues as to what the main idea or theme is. These clues include:
  - ◆ A story with one narrator or one main character may also have one main storyline.
  - ◆ A story with illustrations or pictures that take up most of a page may also have only one storyline.
- Try to recognize the clues about this structure and mark sections of the text that have them.
- When you are finished reading, try to describe the storyline in a few sentences.

Source: © 2021 by Marzano Academies. Adapted with permission.

Figure 2.5: Strategies for addressing main idea items or theme at the fourth-grade level.

The awareness that test items require types of thinking that go beyond the content they purportedly assess changes the relationship between the three types of curriculum. This is depicted in figure 2.6. The major change in the schematic of the three curricula is that the taught curriculum now includes the item-specific thinking skills that are inherent in the items on a test.

An External Test Is the Most Accurate Way to Measure an Individual Student's Knowledge of a Subject Area

The accuracy of external assessments is one of the most misunderstood aspects of measuring students' knowledge of the curriculum. We briefly summarize this issue here; see *Making Classroom Assessments Reliable and Valid* (Marzano, 2018) for a deeper discussion.

As discussed in the first big idea about HRS, the reliability of a test is usually thought of as an indication of the test's accuracy. When large-scale assessments are employed, the reliability of the test is reported as a reliability coefficient, and educators typically assume that if the test has a high reliability coefficient, then the scores individual students receive

Intended Curriculum

Taught Curriculum
(Subject-Specific Knowledge + Item-Specific Thinking Skills)

Assessed Curriculum

Source: © 2021 by Robert J. Marzano.

Figure 2.6: Updated relationship between the three curricula.

are very precise. Surprisingly, this is not the case. A high reliability coefficient for a large-scale assessment provides information about the predictability of *patterns of pairs of scores* as opposed to the precision of individual scores. As an illustration, consider figure 2.7 (page 36).

The scores in figure 2.7 illustrate the exact meaning of the reliability coefficient in a large-scale assessment. To understand it, assume that ten students are administered a test. The three columns after the student numbers represent three hypothetical administrations of the test. For ease of discussion, the scores for the ten students have been listed in rank order. The column titled "Initial Administration" reports the scores of these ten students for the first administration of that test. There is nothing unusual about this administration. Ten students took the test, and raters scored their answers. The other two columns ("Second Administration A" and "Second Administration B") represent two different hypothetical scenarios that measurement experts use to explain the concept of reliability for large-scale assessments.

	Initial Administration	Second Administration A	Second Administration B
Student 1	97	98	82
Student 2	92	90	84
Student 3	86	80	79
Student 4	83	83	72
Student 5	81	79	66
Student 6	80	83	70
Student 7	78	78	66
Student 8	77	74	55
Student 9	70	68	88
Student 10	65	66	78
Reliability Coefficient		0.96	0.32

Source: Adapted from Marzano, 2018.

Figure 2.7: Reliability conceptual model for large-scale assessments.

For this explanation to make sense, you have to assume that the second administration happened right after the initial administration, but somehow students forgot how they answered the items the first time. This, of course, is rather odd and impossible in real life. As strange as this scenario is, it is a basic theoretical underpinning of the traditional concept of reliability. Lee Cronbach and Richard Shavelson (2004) explained this unusual assumption in the following way:

> If hypothetically, we could apply the instrument twice and in the second occasion have the person unchanged and without memory of his first experience, then the consistency of the two identical measures would indicate the uncertainty due to measurement error. (p. 394)

In effect, measurement experts have concluded that if a test is reliable, one would expect students to receive scores on the second administration of the test that are close to the scores they received on the first administration. This is a reasonable assumption and is depicted in the Second Administration A column. It is important to note that all scores in the Second Administration A column are very close to their counterparts in the first administration with two students receiving the same scores. Also note that this pattern of scores for the two administrations has a computed reliability coefficient of 0.96, which is quite high. At a conceptual level, the reliability of a large assessment is defined as the correlation between the first and second administration of a test under the condition that students forgot they had taken the test the first time. An unreliable test under this condition would produce a different pattern of second scores. This is depicted in the Second Administration B column. Notice that students have very different scores on this hypothetical second administration. Also note that the reliability coefficient for that administration is 0.32, which is quite low.

To summarize, if the pattern of scores is the same from one administration of a test to another, then the test is said to be reliable. If the pattern of scores changes from administration to administration, then the test is not considered reliable. As mentioned previously, reliability coefficients range from a 0.00 to a 1.00, with 1.00 meaning that there is no random error operating in an assessment, and 0.00 indicating that the test scores are completely comprised of random error. Psychometrist David Frisbie (1988) asserted that most published tests have reliabilities of about 0.90. From this, one could reasonably conclude that large-scale assessments are very precise. Since then, discussions of the reliability of large-scale assessments have turned more critical of the traditional perspective on the precision of these tests, using arguments similar to that which we present in this text (see also Berman et al., 2020).

The important awareness educators should take away from this discussion is that the reliability coefficient for an external assessment quantifies how much a set of scores for the same students would differ from test administration to test administration, but it provides little information about how precise the scores are for individual students. A test might have a high reliability coefficient but not be very precise in terms of the information it provides about individual students. To obtain a sense of the precision of individual scores, one must think in terms of the standard error of measurement (SEM). The standard error of measurement is a staple of classical test theory. It is based on the assumption that the observed score received by a test-taker is composed of two components: a true score component and an error score component. Of course, this is the basic equation of CTT we discussed previously. A corollary to CTT is that the possible true scores for any given observed scores form a normal distribution around the observed score. The SEM is the standard deviation of the distribution of possible true scores around any given observed score. The SEM provides educators with a sense of the precision of an individual score, whereas the reliability coefficient does not. This is illustrated in figure 2.8.

	Observed Score	Standard Error of Measurement	Range for 68 Percent Confidence	Range for 95 Percent Confidence
0.95	75	1.79	73.21 to 76.79	71.49 to 78.51
0.90	75	2.53	72.47 to 77.53	70.04 to 79.96
0.85	75	3.10	71.90 to 78.10	68.92 to 81.08
0.80	75	3.58	71.42 to 78.58	67.98 to 82.02

Note: The standard deviation of this test was 8.00. The 68 percent confidence interval is calculated by adding and subtracting one SEM from the observed score. The 95 percent confidence interval is calculated by adding and subtracting 1.96 SEM from the observed score.

Figure 2.8: The interpretation of standard error of measurement.

Figure 2.8 depicts the interpretation of the standard error of measurement for a test where students can receive scores that range from 0 to 100. To further illustrate the nature of the SEM, the figure depicts its interpretation for four tests with four different reliability coefficients: 0.80, 0.85, 0.90, and 0.95. If you examine the column titled "Standard Error of Measurement," it is evident that the standard error increases as the reliability coefficient goes down. When a test has a reliability of 0.95, the SEM is 1.79. When a test has a reliability of 0.80, the SEM is 3.58.

The presence of error when interpreting the precision of a score for an individual student comes into sharp focus when you compute confidence intervals around a specific score across the various levels of test reliability. In figure 2.8, we have computed two confidence intervals—the 68 percent confidence interval and the 95 percent confidence interval—at each of the four reliability levels. The 68 percent confidence interval is the range of scores within which you can be about 68 percent sure (that is, confident) that it includes the student's true score. The 95 percent confidence interval is the range of scores within which you can be about 95 percent sure that it includes the student's true score. To illustrate, assume that a student received a score of 75 on the test. When that test has reliability of 0.95, you can be 95 percent sure that the student's true score falls somewhere between 71.49 to 78.51. However, if the test has a reliability of 0.80, you can be 95 percent sure the student's true score falls somewhere between 67.98 to 82.02. These are big differences in ranges. What is probably most shocking to classroom educators is that even when the test has a high reliability of 0.95, the 68 percent confidence interval is 73.21 to 76.79 and the 95 percent confidence interval is 71.49 to 78.51. Even though the overall reliability for the test is quite high, there is still a great deal of imprecision in the score for an individual.

A question that immediately comes up when educators see examples like this is, What is the SEM for common large-scale external tests? For widely used tests, it is relatively easy to determine their SEMs because all testing companies publish these data. A simple internet search will provide such accurate and useful information. For example, the SEM for the SAT is about thirty points for mathematics, evidence-based reading, and writing (The College Board, 2017). Likewise, the typical SEM for the ACT is two to three points for each of the four sections: English, mathematics, reading, and science (ACT, 2023).

HRS and External Assessments

The issues regarding external assessments are some of the more significant problems facing schools. If these issues go unaddressed, a school can do a good job of teaching important content, resulting in substantial learning for students, but not receive enhanced scores on the state test. In the HRS model, this issue is addressed at level 3, a guaranteed and viable curriculum. There are six indicators at this level (Marzano et al., 2014).

3.1 The school curriculum and accompanying assessments adhere to state and district standards.

3.2 The school curriculum is focused enough that teachers can adequately address it in the time they have available.

3.3 All students have the opportunity to learn the critical content of the curriculum..

3.4 The school establishes clear and measurable goals that are focused on critical needs regarding improving overall student achievement at the school level.

3.5 The school analyzes, interprets, and uses data to regularly monitor progress toward school achievement goals.

3.6 The school establishes appropriate school-level and classroom-level programs and practices to help students meet individual achievement goals when data indicate interventions are needed.

It's important to note that the HRS model does not mandate that schools use their state test as the measure of student learning. Although many schools do use their state tests to create level 3 lagging indicators, some use interim assessments employed by the district, and still others seek out specific external tests they believe are aligned to their taught curriculum, even though those tests are not mandated by the state or district. In all cases, at level 3, schools within the HRS process should take great pains to identify the external tests they consider the most accurate and valid measure of both their intended curriculum and their taught curriculum. Of course, a common situation is that schools perceive they have no choice but to use their state test even though they believe it is not aligned adequately with their intended curriculum or their taught curriculum. If this is the case, then there are a series of steps those schools should take.

The first step a school should take is to ensure that it is fully aware of the topics on their state test. To this end, the book *Ethical Test Preparation in the Classroom* (Marzano et al., 2022) can be a useful resource since it identifies the topics in ELA, mathematics, and science that are typically a significant part of external tests. Additionally, it is not uncommon for test publishers to provide lists of the various topics emphasized in specific versions of their test. For example, an elementary school might identify the following fifth-grade mathematics topics as important to their external test.

1. Standard algorithm multiplication
2. Dividing multidigit numbers
3. Solving problems with place value
4. Solving fraction addition and subtraction equations
5. Fraction multiplication with models
6. Interpreting multiplication by fractions
7. Representing quotients as fractions
8. Dividing whole numbers by unit fractions
9. Manipulating decimal place value
10. Addition and subtraction of decimal values
11. Multiplication and division of decimal values
12. Whole number exponents
13. Evaluating powers of 10
14. Numerical expressions
15. Numerical pattern relationships on a coordinate plane
16. Metric and U.S. customary units of measurement
17. Volume of rectangular prisms and solids
18. Two-dimensional figures
19. Graphing points on a coordinate plane

The next step for the school would be to develop a proficiency scale for each topic like that in figure 2.9 for the topic of solving fraction addition and subtraction equations.

4.0	In addition to score 3.0 performance, the student demonstrates in-depth inferences and applications that go beyond what was taught.
3.5	In addition to score 3.0 performance, partial success at score 4.0 content
3.0	The student will: SFASE—Add and subtract fractions with unlike denominators arithmetically (for example, evaluate $\frac{2}{3}+\frac{3}{4}$, $\frac{7}{3}-\frac{9}{6}$, and $2\frac{2}{5}+\frac{1}{2}$).
2.5	No major errors or omissions regarding score 2.0 content, and partial success at score 3.0 content
2.0	SFASE—The student will recognize or recall specific vocabulary (for example, least common multiple) and perform basic processes such as: • Add and subtract fractions with like denominators. • Generate equivalent fractions by multiplying both the numerator and denominator of a given fraction by the same whole number. For example, when given the fraction $\frac{3}{4}$, multiply both the numerator and the denominator by 2 to generate the equivalent fraction $\frac{6}{8}$. • Explain that addition and subtraction of fractions with unlike denominators can be accomplished by converting them to equivalent fractions with a common denominator. • Identify the least common multiple of two whole numbers by counting multiples of the numbers until a common value is found. For example, identify the least common multiple of 5 and 6 by counting in multiples of 5 until arriving at a number that is also a multiple of 6.
1.5	Partial success at score 2.0 content, and major errors or omissions regarding score 3.0 content
1.0	With help, partial success at score 2.0 content and score 3.0 content
0.5	With help, partial success at score 2.0 content but not at score 3.0 content
0.0	Even with help, no success

Source: © 2016 by Marzano Resources. Adapted with permission.

Figure 2.9: Proficiency scale for solving fraction addition and subtraction equations.

When a teacher provides fifth-grade students with a proficiency scale like this, there is no ambiguity regarding the intended curriculum or the taught curriculum. The teacher provides direct instruction regarding the vocabulary and basic facts in the score 2.0 content and offers practice and guidance in the

3.0 content. Thus, the taught curriculum becomes unequivocal. Finally, the content in the proficiency scale would be the basis for all assessments relative to the content in the proficiency scale, rendering the assessed curriculum concrete and focused. In short, the existence of proficiency scales provides complete transparency relative to the intended, taught, and assessed curricula. When proficiency scales are designed with an eye toward the various external tests students will take, students have a clearer picture of what is expected of them in the classroom and on the external test that will be used to make judgments about their proficiency in a given subject area.

Different Expected Test Impacts for Different HRS Levels

From the discussion in the previous section, it is clear that level 3 of the HRS framework has a direct relationship with student achievement as measured by external tests that are valid measures of the taught curriculum. The other levels of the HRS model are focused on other outcomes, all of which are related to student learning but not necessarily to student performance on external tests. This is illustrated in table 2.2. For each level of the HRS framework, the table lists the direct outcomes expected from the programs and practices (that is, leading indicators) that the school has put in place, as well as how these effects ultimately enhance student learning.

Level 3 of the HRS model has the most direct relationship with student learning of subject matter content. As shown in table 2.2, the direct outcomes expected at this level are that teachers have a clear conception of the content to teach and that they craft their lessons using the guidance of the guaranteed and viable curriculum. Additionally, the school sets clear goals for typical (that is, average) student status and growth relative to the taught curriculum. This has the effect of increasing the opportunity for students to learn the taught curriculum, which results in enhanced learning of the same.

At this point, it's important to pay particular attention to the last row of the table, where there is a conditional statement regarding how achieving each HRS level can translate into enhanced scores on external tests. That conditional statement for level 3 is, "If the taught curriculum is aligned with the tested curriculum as measured by an external test, then students' scores on the external test increase." This effect is enhanced if the school teaches the cognitive skills that are specific to the items on the external test. Note that if this condition is not met, students will still have learned the taught curriculum but their learning might not show up as enhanced scores on the external assessments. We believe that there are many schools where students are learning the taught curriculum, but their learning does not manifest as enhanced scores on the test simply because of the lack of overlap between what is tested and what is taught.

Level 1 has a much less direct linkage to student learning. The direct outcomes at this level are that students and teachers have their basic needs met relative to safety, support, and collaboration. These are important outcomes in and of themselves. Because their needs for safety, support, and collaboration are met, teachers can have a better focus on instruction. Similarly, as a result of having their basic needs met, students are better able to focus their attention on the content being taught, which will enhance their learning. But for this to translate into enhanced sores on an external assessment, the taught curriculum must closely align with assessed curriculum as measured by the external assessment.

The path to student learning is more direct at level 2. The direct outcomes at this level are that teachers recognize and utilize the various types of support that are in place to improve their pedagogical skills. As a result of this support, teachers' pedagogical skills improve. Because of enhanced teaching, students have more opportunities to learn the taught curriculum. For this to translate into enhanced performance

Table 2.2: Outcomes for Each Level of the HRS Framework

	Level 1	Level 2	Level 3	Level 4	Level 5
Definition	Programs, practices, and interventions are in place to create a safe, supportive, and collaborative culture.	Programs and practices are in place to promote effective teaching in every classroom.	Programs and practices are in place to develop and utilize a guaranteed and viable curriculum.	Programs and practices are in place to develop and implement a standards-referenced reporting system.	Programs and practices are in place to develop and implement a competency-based system.
Direct Outcomes	• Lagging indicators with concrete and quantitative criteria for developing a safe, supportive, and collaborative culture are met. • Students have their basic needs met relative to safety, support, and collaboration. • Teachers have their basic needs met relative to safety, support, and collaboration. • Teachers can better focus their attention on instruction. • Students can better focus their attention on the taught curriculum. • Student learning of the taught curriculum is enhanced.	• Lagging indicators with concrete and quantitative criteria for enhancing teaching in every classroom are met. • Teachers recognize and utilize the various types of support that are in place to improve their pedagogical skills. • Teachers' pedagogical skills, as employed in the classroom, improve. • Students have greater opportunities to learn the taught curriculum. • Student learning of the taught curriculum is enhanced.	• Lagging indicators with concrete and quantitative criteria for developing and implementing a guaranteed and viable curriculum are met. • Teachers are clear about the content to teach and craft their lessons and units using the guaranteed and viable curriculum. • The school sets clear goals for students' status and growth relative to the guaranteed and viable curriculum. • Students have increased opportunities to learn the taught curriculum. • Student learning of the taught curriculum is enhanced.	• Lagging indicators with concrete and quantitative criteria for implementing a standards-referenced reporting system are met. • Teachers track the growth and status of each individual student on specific topics. • Goals are set and met for the status and growth of individual students. • Students have a clear understanding of what they are expected to know and be able to do. • Individual students' learning of the taught curriculum is enhanced.	• Lagging indicators with concrete and quantitative criteria for implementing a competency-based system are met. • Teachers take collective responsibility for determining each student's status and growth on specific topics. • Students move through the curriculum at a pace consistent with their development and individual needs. • Individual students' learning of the taught curriculum is enhanced. • Students develop an enhanced sense of agency and efficacy.
Condition Required for Enhanced External Assessment Scores	If the taught curriculum is aligned with the tested curriculum as measured by an external test, then students' scores on the external test increase, particularly if students are taught the cognitive skills specific to the external test.	If the taught curriculum is aligned with the tested curriculum as measured by an external test, then students' scores on the external test increase, particularly if students are taught the cognitive skills specific to the external test.	If the taught curriculum is aligned with the tested curriculum as measured by an external test, then students' scores on the external test increase, particularly if students are taught the cognitive skills specific to the external test.	If the taught curriculum is aligned with the tested curriculum as measured by an external test, then scores on the external test increase for targeted students and learning gaps between underserved groups are lessened, particularly if students are taught the cognitive skills specific to the external test.	If the taught curriculum is aligned with the tested curriculum as measured by an external test, then scores on the external test increase for targeted students and learning gaps between underserved groups are lessened, particularly if students are taught the cognitive skills specific to the external test.

on external assessments, other conditions must occur. As with levels 3 and 1, if the taught curriculum is aligned with the tested curriculum as measured by an external test, then students' scores on the external assessment will increase.

At level 4 of the HRS model, the emphasis includes the progress of individual students in addition to the average performance of the school or groups of students within the school. The direct outcomes at this level are that teachers track the growth and status of each student on specific topics and then set and meet specific status and growth goals for individual students. Because of these actions, students have a clear understanding of what they are expected to know and be able to do. This translates into enhanced learning for individual students. While this approach should certainly contribute to the increase in the average scores of students in the school, it will probably more directly help decrease the gaps in scores between those students who come from advantaged backgrounds and those who do not. Some HRS-certified schools have observed these effects even during the school years affected by the COVID-19 pandemic (Kosena & Marzano, 2022). Again, if the taught curriculum is aligned with the tested curriculum as measured by an external test, then scores on the external test will increase for targeted students. This should result in narrowed learning gaps.

At level 5 of the HRS framework, the school's focus includes developing student efficacy and agency while maintaining a focus on academic achievement. A direct outcome of programs and practices at this level is that teachers take collective responsibility for determining each student's status and growth on specific topics. Additionally, at this level, students move through the curriculum at a pace consistent with their development and individual needs. Individual students' learning of the taught curriculum improves, and students develop an enhanced sense of efficacy and agency. If the taught curriculum is aligned with the tested curriculum as measured by an external test, then scores on the external test increase for targeted students and learning gaps between underserved groups are lessened.

To summarize, at all levels of the HRS model, effective execution of the programs and practices important to that level ultimately lead to enhanced student learning of the taught curriculum. Students' learning of the taught curriculum will translate into enhanced scores on an external test *under the condition* that the taught curriculum is aligned with the curriculum assessed by the external test. This fact has strong implications for how schools select the external tests they will use as the criterion measure for their success.

HRS in Practice

There are two primary manifestations of this big idea in schools. One of them focuses on the fact that if schools wish the increased learning of their students to manifest on an external test, then they must ensure that the key topics on the external test are also key topics in the taught curriculum. Some schools go a step further and ensure that students are aware of the requirements for the specific types of items found on the external tests they use.

Some HRS-certified schools, such as John E. Flynn and Sherrelwood Elementary Schools in Westminster, Colorado, have students answer items that are similar to the ones they will find on their state test. Teachers create these items so they deal directly with the content students are working on at that particular point in time. Additionally, students create their own versions of the types of items they will encounter. Finally, teachers challenge students to describe how their self-constructed items could be made easier to answer and how they could be made harder to answer. This asks students to analyze the content at a level usually not required of them by textbook and classroom activities. In another school we have worked with, student-generated items are posted on hallway walls with the names of the student authors on them. Thus, while standing in line in the hallways, students see the items they and their peers have created, which often sparks a discussion of the content.

The second manifestation of this big idea in schools deals with the fact that different levels of the HRS framework have different primary outcomes. This has the effect of reminding administrators, faculty, and staff that student performance on an external test is not the only outcome or perhaps even the most important outcome of schooling. Outcomes like students feeling valued and respected (level 1), teachers developing their pedagogical skills (level 2), students learning academic content in depth (level 3), individual students setting and achieving personal goals regarding specific academic content (level 4), and students developing a strong sense of agency (level 5) are very important outcomes in and of themselves.

Some HRS schools identify individual teachers or groups of teachers whose job it is to champion specific levels of the model. For example, a group of teachers might be selected or volunteer to continually monitor the school's programs and practices for level 1. Those teachers monitor and report on level 1 leading indicators by collecting quick data. Their findings allow the entire school team to recognize progress and accomplishments at level 1 each term. Other levels are monitored and celebrated in the same way. This often occurs as a natural extension of something a group of teachers are already focusing on as part of their professional work. A common example in multiple schools we work with is engaging the group of teachers who make up the positive behavioral interventions and supports (PBIS) team to examine discipline data and PBIS program usage data as a periodic item on their agenda. These teachers systematically collect the quick data in these two categories and report their findings quarterly to the entire faculty, which becomes an opportunity for faculty and staff to celebrate ongoing level 1 milestones and accomplishments. Linden Park Elementary in Idaho Falls, Idaho, has taken an approach where the principal and a team of teachers led initial implementation of level 1 leading indicators and now monitor them while the assistant principal and a separate group of teacher leaders focus on implementing and sustaining the level 2 leading indicators in their school. In the Fullerton School District in California, the teachers on the leadership team of Pacific Drive Elementary developed an HRS handbook that identifies the core systems and practices the school has implemented for levels 1 through 3. The school can use this document to introduce new teachers to the school's HRS systems, and, if need be, a new principal could use it to understand the school's journey and the systems the school currently has in place in each of the first three levels. Such distribution of labor and knowledge ensures that the impact of programs and practices at each level becomes visible, regardless of whether state achievement tests capture it.

Insights and Actions

One major insight relative to this big idea is that external tests just might not be the most valid and reliable measure of student learning in a school. Once educators in a building become aware of this and start to analyze the nature of external tests, they begin to think differently about them. While external tests certainly have their place in the overall feedback loop to schools regarding their students' learning, they are not the best vehicle for feedback at the individual student level. The most common action associated with this awareness is for schools to design systems to evaluate the status of students using homegrown assessments that teachers can employ in classrooms as the primary indictors of student learning. A second major awareness that may result from this big idea is that schools have been ignoring a great deal of evidence that they are accomplishing impressive outcomes outside the arena of performance on external assessments. The action that commonly follows this awareness is a heightened focus on and celebration of those non-assessment-based accomplishments.

Big Idea 3

Schools Must Tailor Programs and Practices to Their Specific Needs

From the discussion of the right work in the introductory chapter, it is clear that the engine of effectiveness in a school is the programs and practices that it employs. Indeed, one might say that one of a school leader's primary jobs is to identify those programs and practices that produce the most powerful results. Within the HRS framework, an important qualifier to this principle is that school leaders commonly must adapt the programs and practices they select or create their own programs and practices. This flies in the face of the common but invalid belief that educational research has already identified *proven practices* that educators can simply take down from the shelf and implement in their schools.

The Importance of Contextualizing Research and Realizing That It Can Be Equivocal

Researchers have warned about using research-based programs in an off-the-shelf manner for decades. For example, in his book *Monitoring School Performance*, Jon Douglas Willms (1992) commented on the massive amount of school effectiveness research (some of which we summarized in the introduction) that came out of the 1970s and 1980s. However, he also offered a warning: "I doubt whether another two decades of research will . . . help us specify a model *for all seasons*—a model that would apply to all schools in all communities at all times" (Willms, 1992, p. 65). In the 1970s, the famous British statistician George Box reportedly (de Leeuw, 2004) said that all models are wrong, but some are useful. Since educational research is based on the use of statistical equations, this is tantamount to saying that all research findings most probably have some error or false assumptions mixed in with their findings. In spite of this, these findings are still useful at the practical level. David Reynolds and Charles Teddlie (2000) offered a similar caution about the use of research findings: "Sometimes the adoption of ideas from research has been somewhat uncritical, for example, the numerous attempts to apply findings from one specific context to another entirely different context when research has increasingly demonstrated significant contextual differences" (p. 216).

Taking a critical eye toward research in terms of its generalizability and validity and considering its specific context are important across fields. When comparing medical research to educational research, Carolyn Riehl (2006) noted:

> When reported in the popular media, medical research often appears as a blunt instrument, able to obliterate skeptics or opponents by the force of its evidence and arguments. . . . Yet repeated visits to the medical journals themselves can leave a much different impression. The serious medical journals convey the sense that medical research is an ongoing conversation and quest, punctuated occasionally by important findings that can and should alter practice, but more often characterized by continuing investigations. These investigations, taken cumulatively, can inform the work of practitioners who are building their own local knowledge bases on medical care. (pp. 27–28)

Within education research, a number of examples have indicated the pitfalls of employing research-based programs and practices without a critical eye to their appropriateness in a local context. Such examples also point out the need for an awareness that typical or average results for an intervention reported in research do not necessarily mean that the intervention always works. Consider the comprehensive school reform movement of the first decade of the 21st century.

The Comprehensive School Reform program was a federally funded initiative that provided grants to schools to adopt evidence-based reform practices (see Borman, Hewes, Overman, & Brown, 2003). The goal of this effort was to provide low-performing schools with research-based approaches to enhancing student achievement. The U.S. Department of Education (2002) defined a comprehensive school reform model in terms of the following characteristics.

- The model has been found through scientifically based research to significantly improve the academic achievement of students.
- The model provides high-quality professional development.
- The model provides for meaningful involvement of parents and community.
- The model employs proven methods for student learning, teaching, and school management.

Intuitively, this seems like a clear path to identifying proven practices that schools can implement to enhance the learning of their students. In the late 1990s and early 2000s, a number of comprehensive school reform models that seemed to possess the required characteristics became popular (see Herman et al., 1999; Northwest Regional Educational Laboratory, 2000). In 2003, Borman and colleagues (2003) reviewed the research on twenty-nine comprehensive school reform models. Their meta-analysis focused on the first criterion, the extent to which scientifically based research indicated that the models improve student achievement. The findings, depicted in table 3.1, provided an interesting perspective. One clear generalization we can infer from these data is that the impact of comprehensive school reform models on student achievement varies considerably.

The standardized mean differences, or effect sizes, reported in table 3.1 range from –2.13 to +7.83. This is a substantial range of outcomes. When one examines what this actually means in terms of the effectiveness of the programs in the study, the conclusions can be surprising and even troublesome. The lowest effect size, –2.13, indicates that the average achievement for students in the experimental group—the school employing the comprehensive school reform model—was 2.13 standard deviations *less* than the average achievement of the school not using the comprehensive school reform approach. In other words,

Table 3.1: Distribution of Effect Sizes for Comprehensive School Reform Models

Effect Size Interval	Percentage of Studies With Results in This Range	Cumulative Percentage
−2.00 to −2.13	0.27	0.27
−1.00 to −1.99	1.50	1.77
−0.01 to −0.99	33.12	34.89
0.00 to 0.99	54.91	89.80
1.00 to 1.99	4.23	94.03
2.00 to 2.99	1.10	95.13
3.00 to 3.99	1.00	96.13
4.00 to 4.99	1.10	97.23
5.00 to 5.99	1.10	98.33
6.00 to 6.99	1.00	99.33
7.00 to 7.83	1.00	100.33

n = 1,111
Percentages do not total 100 due to rounding.

Source: © 2005 by McREL International. Adapted with permission.

the average achievement score for the experimental-group school in this study was at the second percentile of the distribution of achievement scores for the control schools. In contrast, the largest effect size of 7.83 indicates that the average achievement score of the school employing a comprehensive school reform model was 7.83 standard deviations higher than the average score of students in the control group. Stated differently, the average student in the comprehensive school reform group was above the 99.9999999th percentile of the distribution of scores for the control group.

Comprehensive school reform models, then, do not have uniform effects on student learning. Some studies indicate that particular models produce extremely large positive effects on student achievement. Others indicate that a given comprehensive school reform model produces negative effects. In fact, 34.89 percent of the 1,111 effect sizes in Borman and colleagues' (2003) meta-analysis were below zero, indicating that in about 35 percent of the studies reviewed, the schools that did *not* use a given comprehensive school reform model outperformed the schools that did. Taken at face value, these findings should go a long way to shattering any perception that there are *proven* practices that will most certainly work if implemented in any school.

The Borman and colleagues (2003) study also demonstrated some interesting findings regarding how long it takes for a specific intervention to produce stable results:

> After the 5th year of implementation, CSR [comprehensive school reform] effects begin to increase substantially. Schools that had implemented CSR models for 5 years showed achievements that were nearly twice those found for CSR schools in general, and after 7 years of implementation, the effects were more than two and [one] half times the magnitude of overall CSR impact of d = .15 [that is, the standardized mean difference is 0.15]. The small number of schools that had outcome data after 8 to 14 years of CSR model implementation achieved effects that were three and a third times larger than the overall CSR effect. (p. 153)

The average effect size for first-year implementation of comprehensive school reform models was 0.17. The effect sizes for years two, three, and four were 0.14, 0.15, and 0.13, respectively. These are relatively small effect sizes and imply that the effects of comprehensive school reform models are initially quite modest and stay basically the same over the first four years. In the fifth year, the standardized mean difference increases to 0.25, which is certainly an improvement but not a large one. Finally, the effect size increases to a high of 0.50 after the eighth to fourteenth year.

One interpretation of this pattern of effect sizes is that schools must persist in their efforts with any given comprehensive school reform model, expecting relatively small gains for the first four years, after which things will gradually improve. However, another finding from the Borman and colleagues (2003) meta-analysis implies a very different interpretation. The researchers found that staff development support for a given comprehensive school reform model was inversely correlated with the model's effect size. This appears to directly contradict the interpretation that long-term adherence to a comprehensive school reform model will pay off. If this were the case, one would expect that staff development would enhance the impact of a comprehensive school reform model. Borman and colleagues (2003) do not discuss this anomaly. However, a reasonable interpretation is that programs are most effective when they are adapted. That is, it is only when schools adapt a program to their specific situation that it strongly impacts student achievement in a positive way. In our work with school leaders, we have found this to be an operating principle employed by a number of successful administrators. This interpretation is supported by a separate study by researchers Amanda Datnow, Geoffrey D. Borman, Sam Stringfield, Laura T. Overman, and Marisa Costellano (2003) on the impact of comprehensive school reform programs on schools with diverse populations.

Datnow and colleagues (2003) conducted a four-year study of comprehensive school reform implementation in thirteen culturally and linguistically diverse elementary schools. One of the more interesting findings was that a majority of the schools in the study abandoned the comprehensive school reform model they were attempting to implement:

> In summary, at the end of our four-year study, five of the thirteen schools were still continuing to implement their reform designs with moderate to high levels of intensity. Reforms expired in six of thirteen schools we studied; two other schools were still formally associated with their reform but at very low levels. (Datnow et al., 2003, p. 153)

Of the five schools in Datnow and colleagues' (2003) study that persisted with comprehensive school reform implementations, all relied heavily on site-specific adaptations. This does not bode well for a school leader who seeks to rigidly employ an off-the-shelf program or practice.

While the Datnow study dealt exclusively with schools that had culturally and linguistically diverse populations, the research and theory on school change strongly supports the importance of adaptations. Specifically, the work of Gene E. Hall, Shirley M. Hord, and Susan Loucks (Hall & Hord, 1987; Hall, Loucks, Rutherford, & Newlove, 1975; Hord, Rutherford, Huling-Austin, & Hall, 1987) demonstrates that schools must alter the specifics of an innovation to meet the unique needs of their students and community. Indeed, for Hall, Hord, and Loucks, the highest level of implementation of an innovation is defined by adaptation.

The Borman and colleagues (2003) study was conducted two decades prior to the writing of this book. A review of the current extant research can lead one to the same conclusions as those derived at the turn of the century. To illustrate, consider the research from the What Works Clearinghouse (WWC) database, a project of the U.S. Department of Education's Institute of Education Sciences (IES) that was established "to be a central and trusted source of scientific evidence for what works in education" (Wood, 2017, p. 1). While the WWC is an imperfect tool (Wood, 2017), many educators believe its products contain the official recommendations of the U.S. Department of Education. One of the primary tools the WWC employs to make its recommendations useful to educators is an extensive set of practice guides that translate research into practical suggestions. To date, there are twenty-nine practice guides that involve 146 separate recommendations.

Each practice guide lists a number of specific recommendations for K–12 practitioners. What is particularly useful about those recommendations is that each one is coded in terms of the level of research that supports it. To rate the recommendations, IES uses three levels of evidence: strong, moderate, and minimal. The Every Student Succeeds Act (ESSA, 2015) uses another ranking system with four tiers of evidence: tier 1, strong; tier 2, moderate; tier 3, promising; and tier 4, demonstrates a rationale (REL Midwest, 2019). This four-tiered approach aims in part to make research recommendations more interpretable for educators for their site-specific needs. Table 3.2 depicts the distribution of the various levels of evidence across the twenty-nine practice guides and their 146 recommendations.

Table 3.2: Levels of Evidence Across the IES Practice Guides

WWC Criteria				ESSA Criteria			
Levels	n	Percentage	Cumulative Percentage	Levels	n	Percentage	Cumulative Percentage
Strong	41	28.1	28.1	Tier 1	26	17.8	17.8
Moderate	51	34.9	63.0	Tier 2	24	16.4	34.2
Minimal	54	37.0	100.0	Tier 3	42	28.8	63.0
				Tier 4	54	37.0	100.0
Totals	146	100.0		Totals	146	100.0	

Source: Adapted from National Center for Education Evaluation and Regional Assistance, n.d.

The most relevant aspect of these ratings in terms of big idea 3 is that for both the WWC evidence scale and the ESSA evidence scale, the highest category of rigor (that is, *strong* for WWC and *tier 1* for ESSA) applies to relatively few recommendations. Using the WWC scale, only forty-one recommendations (28.1 percent) received the highest rating for rigor; using the ESSA scale, only twenty-six recommendations (17.8 percent) received the highest rating for rigor. Conversely, for both the WWC evidence scale and the ESSA evidence scale, the lowest category of rigor (that is, *minimum* for WWC and *tier 4* for ESSA) applies to the largest numbers of recommendations. Using the WWC scale, fifty-four recommendations (37.0 percent) received the lowest rating for rigor; using the ESSA scale, fifty-four recommendations (37.0 percent) received the lowest rating for rigor.

These findings have profound implications for how educators should think about using research findings. Specifically, the perception that programs and practices listed in the IES practice guides must have a long and consistent history of large, unequivocal effect sizes is not accurate. The IES researchers clearly have taken the position that viable recommendations can be made for a particular program or practice even when there is only minimal research evidence supporting it. If this is true after over twenty years of government-supported research, then schools should feel relatively confident that after a careful review of the extant research and theory, they can generate and carry out recommendations in their schools.

As described in the discussion of the first big idea, the HRS process requires schools to select and implement programs and practices as their leading indicators. But in addition to implementing the selected programs and practices, the HRS process requires leaders to establish criteria for success of these programs and practices. If criteria are not met, the school leaders go back to the programs and practices and make necessary changes to ensure they meet the established criteria. In effect, the HRS process is the tool that helps adapt selected interventions to ensure their success in the local context.

HRS in Practice

The straightforward implication of the equivocal nature of the research in the field of education is that schools should feel free to make adaptations to the programs and practices they use as leading indicators at any given level of the HRS model. This has manifested in many ways within the HRS process. To illustrate, consider leading indicator 1.2: "Students, parents, and the community perceive the school environment as safe, supportive, and orderly." To address this indicator successfully, a school must recognize the unique needs of students, parents, and the community it serves. At Bankhead Middle School in Walker County, Alabama, the school uses its own version of a student mentoring program instead of employing one that was created by someone else. After looking at different options and ideas from existing research-based mentoring program models, the school took specific ideas that matched what they needed to address with their students. Bankhead Middle School principal Amber Freeman explained that meaningful and nurturing relationships are one of the most important things that foster a safe and orderly learning environment. She asserted that their teacher-student mentoring program is the centerpiece of the school philosophy and culture:

> Students are adopted by teachers or other staff and are mentored throughout the year. This relationship-building practice provides an additional layer of support and facilitates the formation of personal connections for at-risk students. As a middle school principal, I understand there is no other time in a child's life (other than birth to one year) that the body goes through a greater phase of physical, emotional, and social development. I have a firm belief that this mentoring program has more of a positive influence on these struggling students than any other single item at our school. When students form a healthy connection with their teachers or other adults in the school, they are more likely to increase their performance in school and make efforts to improve their academics, behavior, and attendance. (A. Freeman, personal communication, April 15, 2022)

The main focus of the mentoring program is to meet mentees' emotional and social needs. Freeman added that the outcomes of building these nurturing relationships include, but are not limited to, improved academic performance and retention rates, improved social and emotional support, enhanced skills and personal growth, and future career success.

The site-designed program is highly nuanced in terms of its defining features. As Freeman explained:

> For this program to be successful, you have to involve the appropriate faculty and staff. These individuals must believe in its importance and fully understand what the mentoring role will require. Most of all, they must love their students. Fortunately, the people that call Bankhead their home are the best in the business. They are possibly the most amazing faculty and staff. They go out of their way to support students and ensure all of their needs

are met. Many of them spend their own money and time to provide extra assistance for students outside of the regular school day. An example of this behavior is exemplified by Mr. Johnson. He coaches for the local parks and rec basketball league. Oftentimes he can be seen in the neighborhoods picking up students to take them to their practices and games. Another teacher, Mrs. Prince, assists a former student by paying her fees to participate in non-school related events, driving her on the weekends to these events, and transporting her to numerous practices. These are just two of hundreds of instances in which the faculty and staff at Bankhead Middle School provide support for our kids to help them to be successful in life. (A. Freeman, personal communication, April 15, 2022)

To be considered for the program, teachers and staff must possess a set of core values and practice certain behaviors. Mentors must love their students and be trustworthy and patient. Mentors must make a commitment to be consistent with meetings and maintain a positive attitude. At all times, faculty and staff must be respectful of students and their needs. This includes having the ability to listen for understanding and communicate effectively at each meeting. Mentors must meet students where they are, but they must also maintain high expectations regarding what they should accomplish over time. Until teachers exhibit these characteristics, they are not considered active mentors in the program. However, they are still an important part of the program by being involved in the mentoring data discussions and examining the effects the program has on the students enrolled in their courses. To date, the mentor program appears to be very malleable to the changing local needs. Freeman noted:

> Our mentoring program, which we feel demonstrates a consistent focus on our student well-being, has been in place for approximately eight years. The mentoring program has changed a bit from year to year. Initially, it was an informal practice of having meaningful conversations with students that needed a little encouragement to get their grades up, improve their attendance rate, or discuss how they could make better choices. It has transformed over the last eight years to a very intentional and deliberate program that provides a missing piece of support for our at-risk students. Procedures for student identification, the assignment of mentors, and careful documentation of meetings are now in place. Careful data collection and analysis have become key components of the mentoring program. This practice not only helps in the decision-making process, but it also serves as an evaluation tool to see what works and what may need to be changed. By using data collected from the program, teachers and students can celebrate successes. The celebration of student achievement and success tends to motivate others. The phrase "success is contagious" holds true here. The data analysis and the proven outcomes of the program can also be used to assist the more reluctant teachers to buy into the mentoring program. These faculty members will see its value and be more likely to get on board. (A. Freeman, personal communication, April 15, 2022)

Finally, Freeman explained that the program they have created has produced tangible results:

> We believe that our mentoring program is continually getting better. One reason is the expectation that we will help our students the absolute best ways we know how. Another reason is the teachers have really embraced the program and the lasting relationships that they have built with their mentees. Lastly, the data show that our specific intent is

creating results with our students. This year's data show that 87 percent of our mentees have improved a letter grade in at least one subject; 68 percent have improved in at least two subjects. Discipline, on average, is less than one referral per student, with 79 percent having no office referrals at all. Attendance has improved by 6.36 days per year per student in the program. (A. Freeman, personal communication, April 15, 2022)

Bankhead Middle School is an enduring example of how a school can create a program that meets its specific needs and continue to develop and adapt that program over a number of years.

Insights and Actions

The most common insight from this big idea is that research results are certainly a good place to start to identify programs and practices to employ, but schools must make adaptations even to evidence-based initiatives. Another awareness is that it takes a significant amount of time—measured in years—to ensure that programs and practices are having their full impact on students. Probably the most salient action emanating from this big idea is that schools tend to rely more and more on programs and practices that they create themselves, commonly using pieces and parts of other programs and practices.

Big Idea 4

Without Adequate Focus and Energy, Even Effective Programs and Practices Will Start to Degrade

It is easy—perhaps even a natural human tendency—to stop thinking about programs and practices that are in place and have demonstrated their effectiveness. But a central characteristic of a high reliability organization is that it continually monitors the level of effectiveness of even its proven programs and practices. The trap that many schools fall into involves the assumption that programs and practices that are operating successfully at one point in time will continue to produce their intended effects in the future without much maintenance. Stated differently, once a school has determined that its interventions are meeting the criteria in the lagging indicators, it would be a serious mistake to assume that those programs and practices will continue to produce the same results indefinitely. Such assumptions open the door to entropy.

Entropy

Entropy is a concept that originated in the field of thermodynamics. The genesis of the idea and the term *entropy* itself are credited to the second law of thermodynamics and Rudolf Clausius in the middle of the 19th century. Héctor A. Martínez-Berumen, Gabriela C. López-Torres, and Laura Romo-Rojas (2014) explained, "Clausius developed the concept based on the formulation of the second law of thermodynamics, which states that, without outside intervention, heat always flows from a warm body to a body with lower temperature" (p. 390). In a more general context, *entropy* refers to the condition in which a system naturally begins to lose energy and move toward ineffectiveness or disorder over time. Writing for the *Journal of Humanistic Mathematics*, Philip J. Davis (2011) noted, "an increase of entropy means an increase of disorder, dissipation and decay" (p. 119). Social science researchers assert that entropy exists in social systems just as it does in thermodynamic systems. Martínez-Berumen and colleagues (2014) discussed the role of entropy in social systems:

> An organization is conceived of as a system, described as a combination of assembled and interconnected elements, forming an organized set, which have a defined goal, and are immersed in an environment with which they interact. Since organizational design and management integrates various factors and perspectives, both internal and external,

including technical and technological, cultural, social, political and economic, it is possible to apply a systems approach, and systems engineering concepts, to study this kind of systems. (p. 391)

When social systems are implemented, specific factors naturally influence the systems and make them subject to entropy. Thomas Mavrofides, Achilleas Kameas, Dimitris Papageorgiou, and Antonios Los (2011) identified a number of factors that contribute to the existence of entropy in social organization systems and described the first two as follows:

(1) Systems are solutions. No solution can have a substantial meaning unless there is a problem (or a class of problems) defined. (2) Systems are problems for their environments. Every time a system emerges, its environment faces a rise in complexity and reacts by upgrading its own complexity. (p. 10)

These two factors shed light on why entropy threatens every system an organization implements. First, the system exists to address problems or potential problems. Second, implementing the system increases the complexity of the organization. The reality is a system that works well in the first year or two can quickly become at risk for disorder. Kenneth D. Bailey (2008) spoke directly to this fact: "It is theoretically possible (but highly unlikely) that a social system could exist in a permanently open state" (p. 590–591). Because of this fact, organizations must ask themselves, How can we combat entropy in our systems? Proactively addressing this question is a characteristic of a high reliability organization. Martínez-Berumen and colleagues (2014) also spoke to this concept: "A sustainable system must, by definition, ensure that its level of entropy does not increase to maximum levels, since maximum entropy (characterized by absolute homogeneity) means the system death" (p. 396).

Entropy in organizational initiatives is so common that social science researchers use a model known as the sigmoid curve to visualize the phenomenon (Hipkins & Cowie, 2016). This is depicted in figure 4.1. A number of theorists have used the sigmoid curve or a variation of it to describe the process of implementing or learning something new (for example, Adizes, 1990; Handy, 1995; Rogers, 2003). The sigmoid curve is an S-shaped curve that models stages of implementation of a new program or practice. There are three phases in the curve: the learning phase, the growth phase, and the decline phase. The learning phase is represented by the initial section of the curve and shows a dip in performance before starting to rise. This implementation dip is common when organizations implement new initiatives. The growth phase is where the program or practice demonstrates perceptible evidence and results. The growth phase can continue for a long period of time. Unfortunately, if the health of the system is not monitored and managed, entropy begins to occur and the system moves into the decline phase. The decline phase of the curve indicates the system is experiencing some level of entropy. If the errors are not addressed, the system will continue to fall further into disorder, which can result in a total system failure.

The phases in the sigmoid curve correlate to the five levels in the HRS leadership accountability scales introduced in big idea 1 (see figure 1.1, page 15). The growth phase of the sigmoid curve correlates to the developing and applying levels. The top of the growth curve represents programs and practices being in place and the lagging indicator data showing the system is healthy and fulfilling its purpose. This correlates to the sustaining level of the HRS leadership scale. At the sustaining level, the leader's goal is to prevent the system slipping into the decline phase as entropy tries to take hold. To combat the inevitable creep of entropy into their systems, High Reliability Schools engage in two salient behaviors: they continually and systematically collect data and they continually and systematically develop and refine procedures.

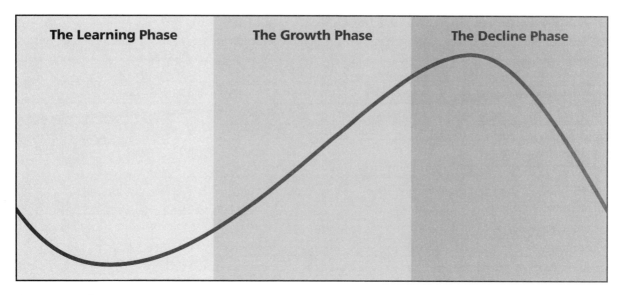

The Learning Phase   **The Growth Phase**   **The Decline Phase**

Source: Warrick, 2020, p. 315.

Figure 4.1: Three phases of the sigmoid curve concept.

Continuous and Systematic Data Collection

As explained in big idea 1 (page 13), data collection is built into the HRS certification process. For example, schools must collect survey data right from the outset to establish a baseline regarding their current status for each leading indicator within an HRS level, collect more data to measure the impact of the programs and practices they implement, and then continue collecting quick data to ensure implementation does not degrade. This offers opportunities to identify entropy within existing systems. Consider the example HRS survey results in figure 4.2 (page 56) for leading indicator 1.7, which deals with the acknowledgment of individuals and the school as a whole.

The survey data clearly indicate differences in perception for this leading indicator between stakeholder groups. School administrators indicated strong agreement with all the survey items related to leading indicator 1.7, reflected in the mean scores of 5. The mean scores among teachers and staff range from 3.37 to 3.68, indicating neutral to moderate agreement. Parent and guardian mean scores show slightly stronger agreement with the statements, ranging from 3.63 to 3.95. The mean score for students is only 2.86 for this leading indicator. Looking deeper into the data, the student mode was 4; the notable difference between the mean and the mode suggests outliers in the student data. This is also signaled by the large standard deviation of 1.34.

Given the focus of leading indicator 1.7, the survey data indicate something might be amiss in the system relative to acknowledging individuals and the school as a whole. School leaders might reasonably conclude that entropy is in play. The good news is that now the school is aware of the issue and can address this indicator as a focus for school improvement.

Systematic collection of data can also provide a school information about its current status on the sigmoid curve as it relates to the implementation of specific programs and practices. Using quick data (as introduced in big idea 1, page 13) provides a vital information loop so that if errors are beginning to occur, those errors can be addressed before they become systemwide failures. This leadership action

Table 14: Descriptive Statistics for Leading Indicator 1.7 (Administrator)

Survey Item	M	SD	Mode	n
Our school's accomplishments have been adequately acknowledged and celebrated.	5.00	0.00	5	2
Teacher teams' or departments' accomplishments have been adequately acknowledged and celebrated.	5.00	0.00	5	2
Individual teachers' accomplishments have been adequately acknowledged and celebrated.	5.00	0.00	5	2
I acknowledge and celebrate individual accomplishments, teacher-team or department accomplishments, and whole-school accomplishments in a variety of ways (for example, through faculty celebrations, newsletters to parents, announcements, the school website, or social media).	5.00	0.00	5	2
I regularly celebrate the successes of individuals in a variety of positions in the school (such as teachers or support staff).	5.00	0.00	5	2

Note: M = arithmetic mean; SD = standard deviation; Mode = most common response(s); n = valid response count

Table 15: Descriptive Statistics for Leading Indicator 1.7 (Teachers and Staff)

Survey Item	M	SD	Mode	n
Our school's accomplishments have been adequately acknowledged and celebrated.	3.68	1.04	4	68
My team's or department's accomplishments have been adequately acknowledged and celebrated.	3.37	1.17	4	65
My individual accomplishments have been adequately acknowledged and celebrated.	3.42	1.18	4	67
School leaders acknowledge and celebrate individual accomplishments, teacher-team or department accomplishments, and whole-school accomplishments in a variety of ways (for example, through faculty celebrations, newsletters to parents, announcements, the school website, or social media).	3.51	1.24	4	67
School leaders regularly celebrate the successes of individuals in a variety of positions in the school (such as teachers or support staff).	3.43	1.25	4	65

Note: M = arithmetic mean; SD = standard deviation; Mode = most common response(s); n = valid response count

Table 14: Descriptive Statistics for Leading Indicator 1.7 (Parent/Guardian)

Survey Item	M	SD	Mode	n
The accomplishments of my child's school have been adequately acknowledged and celebrated.	3.79	1.14	4	77
The accomplishments of my child's teachers have been adequately acknowledged and celebrated.	3.68	1.08	4	63
My child's individual accomplishments have been adequately acknowledged and celebrated.	3.63	1.23	4	83
The leaders of my child's school acknowledge and celebrate individual accomplishments, teacher-team or department accomplishments, and whole-school accomplishments in a variety of ways (for example, through faculty celebrations, newsletters to parents, announcements, the school website, or social media).	3.95	1.12	4	74

Note: M = arithmetic mean; SD = standard deviation; Mode = most common response(s); n = valid response count

Table 15: Descriptive Statistics for Leading Indicator 1.7 (Student)

Survey Item	M	SD	Mode	n
When I achieve a goal or accomplish something important, my school's leaders, my teachers, and other students celebrate it.	2.86	1.34	4	194

Note: M = arithmetic mean; SD = standard deviation; Mode = most common response(s); n = valid response count

Source: © 2022 by Marzano Resources. Used with permission.

Figure 4.2: Indicator 1.7 survey results for administrators, teachers and staff, parents and guardians, and students.

allows the school to avoid the decline phase. Figure 4.3 shows the concept of quick data in relationship to the growth and decline phases of the sigmoid curve. Point A in the growth curve represents where quick data begin to indicate there are issues of concern in system performance. The two divergent lines represent the two ways leaders might respond: continuing on the same trajectory and ultimately falling into decline, or using quick data to address the issues before they become systemwide failures and in so doing, successfully combating entropy in the system.

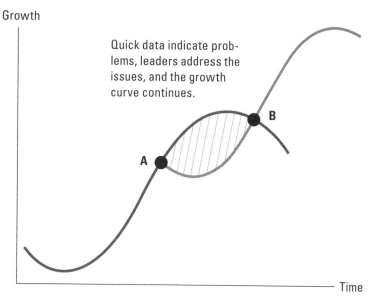

Source: Warrick, 2020, p. 320.

Figure 4.3: Quick data correlating to the growth and decline phases of the sigmoid curve.

One of the most common questions regarding the use of quick data is, How often should it be collected? Schools can answer this question by first thinking about what programs or practices they want to monitor and how long they have been functioning successfully. For example, assume that in the first week of the school year, the school implemented a system of practices to address leading indicator 1.1 (The faculty and staff perceive the school environment as safe, supportive, and orderly) and bring more order to how students move through the hallways during passing time. Leaders set the lagging indicator criterion as a 20 percent reduction in discipline infractions occurring during passing periods compared to the previous year. The administration monitors hallway infractions, and, in November, the school reaches this goal. At this point, the system of practices is functioning as intended. However, it is still very early in the life of those practices, so they need frequent monitoring. The school should gather quick data over relatively short increments of time, perhaps every other week for a few months, to ensure this system continues to work as intended. If quick data indicate the system is functioning consistently over time, the school might move to quick data reviews every six weeks.

In other words, the nature and frequency of quick data collection vary according to the purpose of the practice in question and in conjunction with the longevity of health in the system. The appendix (page 85) includes multiple examples of quick data sources a school might use to monitor different systems within each leading indicator. However, the examples we have provided are not the only types of quick data a school might use. A school can decide what quick data they will gather by considering two questions: (1) What is the purpose of the system being monitored? and (2) What will tell us if it is working?

Another key aspect of quick data monitoring is that it should not be the responsibility of school administrators only. A school's faculty and staff can and should be involved in the collection of quick data, as can students and parents. *A Handbook for High Reliability Schools* (Marzano et al., 2014) uses the example of a *foreign objects and debris (FOD) walk* aboard an aircraft carrier to demonstrate this point. During a FOD walk, personnel on the aircraft carrier walk along the deck shoulder to shoulder, picking up anything they find to make landing on and taking off from the flight deck safer for jets and the aviators who fly them. The salient point here is the FOD walks require all available members of a ship's crew to work together to identify and alleviate a potential future problem.

FOD walks are a metaphor for how HRS schools can and should operate. Consider the scenario of a school implementing leading indicator 2.1: "The school communicates a clear vision as to how teachers should address instruction." Assume the school reaches the criterion for this lagging indicator, which is that 90 percent of teachers are using elements of the instructional model 90 percent of the time based on classroom-walkthrough-observation data and artifacts of instructional practice. School administrators now have several options for quick data monitoring to combat entropy in this system. First, they can continue to periodically review the percentage of instructional model elements usage based on walkthrough-observation data. Additionally, administrators could ask collaborative team leaders or department chairs to engage in quick discussions with their colleagues to capture data regarding the use of specific elements of the instructional model. These quick-data discussions could occur with whatever frequency the school leadership deems necessary—perhaps quarterly. Likewise, school administrators could administer a short survey every six weeks to ask random teachers what specific elements of the model they are using currently and how they are using them. Involving teacher leaders and using multiple sources of data allow school leaders to efficiently monitor the usage of their model of instruction.

When examining quick data, one of two situations might reveal itself and inform school leaders' subsequent actions. The first situation is that there are problems beginning to occur. Again using indicator 2.1 to illustrate, assume the quick data indicate that teachers new to the school are not using the specific elements of the instructional model and are unaware of some of the elements within the instructional model. Because continuous and systematic data collection made this problem apparent in a timely manner, school leaders can address the problem with interventions to build the capacity of new teachers to the school.

The second scenario is that quick data clearly indicate the programs and practice in question are functioning as intended. Appropriate reactions to this result could include open acknowledgment of success for the whole school. In general, schools often miss opportunities to acknowledge well-functioning systems of operation. Quick data can provide the rationale and specificity for acknowledgments directed at doing the right work. Such acknowledgment can keep a school on a growth trajectory relative to a specific program or practice. Author and coaching expert Judith E. Glaser (2017) addressed the power of celebration as a leadership action: "Great leaders identify, measure, recognize, and reward meaningful efforts and achievements—and *celebrate often* with the people involved. . . . Creating a feeling of celebration helps meet people's needs for inclusion, innovation, appreciation, and collaboration." When quick data indicate success in sustaining a leading indicator schoolwide, HRS leaders should share these data with staff and stakeholders and seize these opportunities to build support for sustaining the systems of operation.

Continuous and Systematic Use of Procedures

The second process HRS schools use to combat entropy is to continually and systematically design and execute procedures. Many industries outside of education that strive for high reliability status use procedures as the bedrock of their programs and practices. Arguably it was the surgeon Atul Gawande who brought the importance of procedures to the attention of the general public. In his 2007 book *Better: A Surgeon's Notes on Performance*, Gawande argued that procedures are necessary for many medical interventions, ranging from surgeries to administering medication. He emphasized the importance of continually refining and improving procedures through analytical collaboration among physicians. In his 2009 book *The Checklist Manifesto: How to Get Things Right*, Gawande included the use of checklists as a crucial aspect of procedures in medicine and other fields. Gawande (2009) explained that checklists can help reduce errors in complex, high-stakes situations, such as surgery or aviation. He noted that even highly skilled professionals can make mistakes or overlook important steps in a procedure, and checklists can serve as an important reminder of all critical steps.

The tendency to generate procedures is a natural human phenomenon. In 2012, Charles Duhigg published *The Power of Habit: Why We Do What We Do in Life and Business*, which explores the science behind habits and how they shape our daily lives. In effect, habits are systems of procedures and checklists that people might never write down or even describe verbally, but they execute them in specific situations without consciously thinking about them. Habits can be positive because they allow us to engage in relatively complex tasks without taking up much of our working memory. This makes it possible for us to think of other things while engaged in routine behaviors. However, habits can be negative because they are very difficult to change even when they are harmful to us. One of Duhigg's (2012) more powerful insights is the concept of *keystone habits*, or habits that have ripple effects on other areas of our lives. For example, exercising can be a keystone habit because it can lead to better eating habits and improved productivity at work.

In addition to the ingrained procedures of habits, formal procedures have a long history as well, dating back at least a few millennia. For example, archaeologists have found ancient Egyptian texts from 1550 BC describing medical procedures for eye surgery and hernias (Metwaly et al., 2021; Todd, 1921). In law, formal procedures for resolving legal disputes, including rules for gathering evidence, conducting trials, and imposing punishments, go back to the Code of Hammurabi, which dates to 1750 BC in Babylon (Slanski, 2012). In the modern world, procedures are ubiquitous. In the realm of naval aviation, there is a Naval Air Training and Operating Procedures Standardization (NATOPS) manual for every plane a Navy pilot learns to fly. The NATOPS manual provides detailed instructions for the safe operation of a specific aircraft. It details procedures for takeoff and landing, in-flight maneuvers, and emergency procedures. Prior to actually flying any new type of plane, Navy aviators attend intense classes (referred to as *ground school*) in which they must demonstrate that they know each procedure in the NATOPS manual. Interestingly, Naval aviators have a saying, "NATOPS manuals are written in blood." By this, they mean that anytime an accident occurs resulting in damage to the plane or injury or death to the pilot, new procedures are created to ensure that the accident does not occur again, and those procedures are added to the current NATOPS manual (T. Marzano, personal communication, 2018).

The concept of procedures is also foundational to the development of models of human thinking and ultimately of artificial intelligence (AI). Cognitive psychologist John Anderson (1976, 1983, 1990, 1993) is a pioneer in the field of artificial intelligence. He characterized procedures as sets of production rules, which involve a set of *if-then* statements that describe the relationship between an input or a stimulus and an action or a response. Production rules are the basis for virtually all human behaviors. For example, when driving a car, one of the production rules we no doubt employ might be stated as, *if* the traffic light is green, *then* accelerate. Another production rule used when driving might be, *if* the car in front of me stops suddenly, *then* apply the brakes. Anderson (1993) further explained that the human mind consists of a myriad of interacting and overlapping production systems. Each production system is made up of production rules that are activated when a particular stimulus is detected. In actual practice, these production systems are extremely specific in terms of the elements in the if-then statements and how these statements are related. To illustrate, consider figure 4.4, containing a production system for the mathematical process of adding two numbers.

NEXT-COLUMN:

IF the goal is to solve an addition problem and c1 is the rightmost column without an answer digit

THEN set a subgoal to write out an answer in c1

PROCESS-COLUMN:

IF the goal is to write out an answer in c1, and d1 and d2 are the digits in that column and d3 is the sum of d1 and d2

THEN set subgoal to write out d3 in c1

WRITE ANSWER-CARRY

IF the goal is to write out d1 in c1 and there is an unprocessed carry in c1 and d2 is the number after d1

THEN change the goal to write out d2 and mark the carry as processed

---

Source: Adapted from Anderson, 1993, p. 5.

Figure 4.4: Production system for adding two numbers.

Anderson (1993) explains the flow of action in these production rules as follows:

> The production rules are organized around a set of goals. One goal is always active at any point in time. The first production rule, NEXT-COLUMN, focuses attention on the rightmost unprocessed column and will start by choosing the ones column. The next production to apply is PROCESS-COLUMN. It responds to the goal of adding the column digits, but there are other elements in its condition. The second clause, "d1 and d2 are in that column," retrieves the digits. Its third clause, "d3 is the sum of d1 and d2," matches the sum of those digits. In its action, it sets the subgoal of writing out d3. (p. 5)

This figure is intended to demonstrate how intricate and detailed procedures are whether they are found in computer simulations of what human beings do (as is the case with figure 4.4) or in the human mind. Effective procedures tell what specific actions to take in specific situations. Anderson's notion of production rules has been applied to a wide range of domains, including language learning, problem solving, and decision making. It is an important concept in cognitive psychology, as it helps to explain how humans are able to learn and execute complex behaviors in a flexible and adaptive manner.

Procedures are certainly not strangers in the classroom either. Teachers use them in the form of standard operating procedures for behavior, steps for performing academic tasks, and so on. For example, consider the following procedure for reading a bar graph a teacher might provide fourth-grade students.

Step 1.   Look at the title of the bar graph and try to remember what you already know about the topics the graph includes.

Step 2.   Remind yourself that a bar graph illustrates the quantities of two or more types of things.

Step 3.   Look at the horizontal axis and identify the various types of things each bar represents.

Step 4.   Look at the vertical axis and identify the scale used in the bar graph. What is the lowest score on the scale, and what is the highest score on the scale?

Step 5.   For each bar, identify the score or quantity associated with it using the vertical axis.

From this discussion, it is clear that procedures are and always have been central to the efficacy and efficiency of many endeavors. Indeed, they are central to human thinking and behavior. Without the development of new procedures, there is no development within a domain. Quite obviously, leaders within effective schools have developed procedures without the use of the HRS process. But the HRS process elevates the design of procedures to a new level of awareness for school leaders. One might say that the HRS process conveys the message that designing and monitoring the execution of procedures is one of the most important jobs of a school leader. They must create procedures to ensure implementation of the leading indicators, and they must create procedures to bolster the effectiveness of their programs and practices when data indicate they are not producing their desired effects.

HRS in Practice

In HRS schools, establishing and maintaining focus and energy to ensure that even effective programs and practices do not degrade are commonly embedded in large-scale schoolwide initiatives. For example, at Westwood High School in Austin, Texas, school leaders, teachers, and staff, with input from the student body and school community, have implemented flexible scheduling to support their standards-referenced grading system (HRS level 4) as well as their data collection to create a schoolwide intervention system.

Westwood High School states the purpose of its flexible scheduling system, referred to as *Flextime*, as follows:

> Westwood High School provides opportunities for students to build academic autonomy and college/career-readiness skills. We recognize that student stress is a universal problem and a concern in our community. Flexible time during the school day will facilitate academic success and reduce student stress by providing access to teachers outside of the traditional schedule. Additionally, Flextime will provide students with opportunities to master critical academic skills, develop non-academic interests and career readiness skills, and foster a sense of community. (Westwood High School, personal communication, 2020)

The tacit wish of Westwood educators was to create a broad-based intervention that would address a number of their goals in such a way that it allowed for the collection of data relative to the status of those goals, and those data could then be used to make judgments about procedures that should be changed or tweaked within the system. The Westwood High School Flextime period is a forty-minute block scheduled into each school day. Figure 4.5 (page 62) and figure 4.6 (page 63) provide sample scheduling details for Flextime.

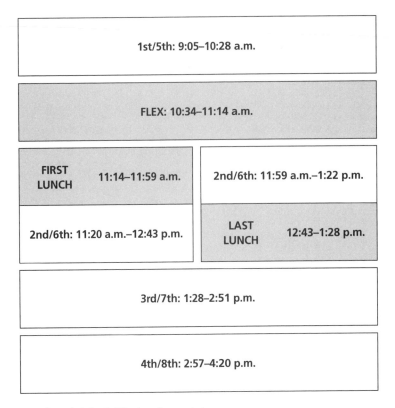

Figure 4.5: Westwood High School bell schedule.

Figures 4.5 and 4.6 provide the general structure of the Flextime schedule, but it is how the schedule is used that discloses its true power. Students are assigned to a different homeroom class each day. This homeroom class is rotated daily so that by default all students will have extra learning time with each of the teachers on their course schedule at least once during a two-week period. Furthermore, students are provided the opportunity to use a web-based student management system to either stay in their homeroom class or self-select into a different teacher's room each day during Flextime. Students are allowed to select any teacher's room to attend if the teacher has available seats. In this way, students have a level of autonomy to select what type of support they need, when they get it, and from which teacher.

Given the fact that all students can seek extra support from any one of their teachers, the Flextime intervention structure requires a mindset of collective ownership for student success from school staff members. As Anthony Muhammad (2015) declared, to attempt to close the achievement gap and support all students, educators must possess an "unwavering set of collective beliefs and actions rooted in the goal of achieving high levels of academic and social success for all students despite internal or external barriers" (p. 92). Foundational to the success of this schoolwide intervention structure is the fact that the staff believe that each member is available for and plays an active role in every student's academic success and social-emotional well-being.

Beyond the expressed intent to relieve student academic stress and cultivate academic autonomy in students, Westwood High School uses Flextime to intervene with specific students who have academic, social-emotional, or behavioral support needs. For academics, Westwood teachers and collaborative teams use classroom standards-based practices to determine whether students are falling or have fallen behind in

Fall 2021 Flex Schedule

Monday	Tuesday	Wednesday	Thursday	Friday	Monday	Tuesday	Wednesday	Thursday	Friday
8/16	8/17	8/18 Homeroom No Flex	8/19	8/20	10/18	10/19	10/20	10/21	10/22
			No Flexing Out - Training		Academic	Academic	Academic	Academic	Clubs & Interest Groups
8/23	8/24	8/25	8/26	8/27 Pep Rally	10/25	10/26	10/27	10/28	10/29
	No Flexing Out - Training				Academic	Academic	Academic	Academic	Clubs & Interest Groups
8/30	8/31	9/1	9/2	9/3	11/1 Student Holiday	11/2	11/3	11/4	11/5
Academic	Academic	Academic	No Flexing Out -Training	Clubs & Interest Groups		Academic	Academic	Academic	
9/6	9/7	9/8	9/9	9/10	11/8	11/9	11/10	11/11	11/12
	Academic	Academic	Academic	Academic	Academic	Academic	Academic	Academic	Clubs & Interest Groups
9/13	9/14	9/15	9/16	9/17	11/15	11/16	11/17	11/18	11/19
Academic	Academic	Academic	Academic	Clubs & Interest Groups	Academic	Academic	Academic	Academic	Clubs & Interest Groups
9/20	9/21	9/22	9/23	9/24	11/22	11/23	11/24	11/25	11/26
Academic	Academic	Academic	Academic	Clubs & Interest Groups		Thanksgiving holiday!			
9/27 Student Holiday	9/28	9/29	9/30	10/1	11/29	11/30	12/1	12/2	12/3
	Academic	Academic	Academic		Academic	Academic	Academic	Academic	Clubs & Interest Groups
10/4	10/5	10/6	10/7	10/8	12/6	12/7	12/8	12/9	12/10 C Day No Flex
Academic	Academic	Academic	Academic	Clubs & Interest Groups	Academic	Academic	Academic	Academic	
10/11 Student Holiday	10/12	10/13	10/14	10/15	12/13	12/14	12/15	12/16	12/17 Student Holiday
	Academic		Academic	Academic		FINALS - No Flex			

Source: © 2021 by Westwood High School. Used with permission.

Figure 4.6: Flextime calendar.

their course-level academic targets. The staff uses the Flextime protocols to mandate academic intervention for specific students. All teachers across a common content area use Flextime to facilitate the ongoing reteaching and reassessing of students who have not yet mastered the critical content for each content area. For social-emotional and behavioral needs, the campus intervention team examines student behavior data, mental health referrals, social need referrals, and teacher recommendations to activate mandatory supports during the Flextime period. School counselors, social workers, and administrators conduct mental health support sessions, restorative discipline conferences, and social wellness sessions involving students, their families, and community resources during the Flextime period. The school also uses Friday Flextime to provide all students with exposure to career and life readiness skills, develop nonacademic interests, and foster a sense of community. In aggregate, Westwood educators have created implicit and explicit procedures for a wide array of Flextime situations, some of which are listed in figure 4.7.

In effect, at Westwood, the Flextime schedule is an overarching initiative that requires the design and use of multiple procedures. These procedures are designed to produce a continuous flow of data that helps monitor how well the system is functioning and generates changes through the creation of new procedures when leaders determine that the system is not functioning as intended. This is not an unusual approach in HRS schools.

Insights and Actions

Perhaps the overarching insight from this big idea is that getting a school to the level of high reliability status requires energy and focus that never subside. Effective schooling is always hard work and never gets easy, as evidenced by the need to continuously collect data and develop and monitor procedures. Interestingly, along with this awareness is a recognition of the nobility of hard work and the inherent heroism of the countless administrators, teachers, and staff members throughout K–12 education who dedicate their lives to this endeavor on a daily basis. Probably the most salient action is that educators in the HRS process come to work with renewed energy and dedication to this noble and heroic endeavor of the schooling the youth they work with. The realization that the hard work they do produces concrete results in students provides educators with an inspirational lens through which to view the tasks in front of them.

1. Student versus staff choice
   a. Level 1: Procedures that allow students to stay in their home Flex or flex out as desired
   b. Level 2: Procedures for teachers to contact parents if they have a student who needs to "flex in" beyond home Flex
   c. Level 3: Procedures for administrators and counselors to consult with teachers to develop an academic, behavior, and social success plan requiring students to attend mandatory Flex intervention

2. Academic versus club time
   a. Monday–Thursdays = academics
      i. Procedures for college visits
   b. Fridays:
      i. Procedures for interest group or club days
      ii. Procedures for nonmandatory meetings
      iii. Procedures for teacher-designed activities
      iv. Procedures for pep rallies
      v. Procedures for class meetings (graduation meetings, senior photo, and so on)
   c. Procedures for shortened weeks; Friday becomes an academic Flex day

3. Prescribed time versus open tutorial time
   a. Procedures for teacher-conference Flextimes
   b. Procedures for open tutoring
   c. Procedures for extension lessons
   d. Procedures for reteaching
   e. Procedures for connecting with students
   f. Procedures for academic counseling
   g. Procedures for make-up quizzes or tests

4. Student sign-up deadline
   a. Procedures for 9:05 a.m. sign-up deadline
   b. Procedures for students' Flextime sign-up
   c. Teacher procedures for creating Flextime sessions

5. Classroom expectations
   a. Teacher-designed procedures for students regarding classroom behavior during Flextime
   b. Procedures for how and when clubs and special interest groups will mesh with Flextime schedule
   c. Procedures for substitute teachers during Flextime

6. Non-negotiables
   a. Procedures for student attendance at Flextime sessions: no passes to other teachers, alpha offices, library, vending machines, locker rooms, cafeteria, cars, and so on
   b. Procedures for content addressed in Flextime sessions: not a time for new instruction or presentation of new material
   c. Procedures for calling students out of Flextime: staff cannot call students out of Flex (counselors, alpha offices, and so on).
   d. Procedure for counselors: can open up seats to see students. If students sign up, they must stay in the alpha office the entire Flex block. Other alpha office errands are not allowed. Flextime is also important operational time for alpha offices.
   e. Procedures for bathroom and water breaks during Flextime: only allow one student out at a time for restroom or water fountain.

7. Accountability
   a. Procedures for report generation: administration will run attendance reports on a regular basis and assign consequences for students.
   b. Procedures for report generation on individual students: let administration know about special circumstance students.

Source: © 2021 by Westwood High School. Used with permission.

Figure 4.7: Areas for which Westwood High School has created implicit and explicit procedures.

Big Idea 5

Standards-Referenced Reporting and Competency-Based Education Are at the Top of the HRS Framework Because of Their Magnitude of Change and Their Focus on Equity

Since the inception of the HRS framework (Marzano et al., 2014), it has not been uncommon for educators to ask why level 4, standards-referenced reporting, and level 5, competency-based education, are at the top of the framework. The answer is not because they are better than the other levels, although they do provide options that are not available within the other levels. They are at the top of the framework primarily for two reasons: (1) they require second-order change, or a substantive paradigm shift, for school systems; and (2) they have structural features that orient schools toward equity.

Second-Order Change

Standards-referenced reporting and competency-based education represent major changes in the way schools are organized, how staff interact with students and parents, and what they expect from students and parents. If a school tried to undertake such major changes without securing effective programs and practices in levels 1, 2, and 3 of the HRS model, the changes required by levels 4 and 5 would likely result in significant upheavals in the school. Stated more technically, levels 4 and 5 are typically second-order change for most school systems.

The concept of second-order change is well established in the literature on leadership (see Argyris & Schön, 1974, 1978; Heifetz, 1994) and a variety of other domains (Ertmer, 1999; Witkin, 2014). In the books *School Leadership That Works* (Marzano, Waters, & McNulty, 2005) and *District Leadership That Works* (Marzano & Waters, 2009), Marzano and colleagues applied the research and theory on first- and second-order change to K–12 schooling. Some of the important characteristics of first-order versus second-order change are depicted in table 5.1 (page 68).

Table 5.1: Characteristics of First-Order Change Versus Second-Order Change

First-Order Change	Second-Order Change
Is perceived as an extension of the past	Is perceived as a break with the past
Fits within existing paradigms	Lies outside existing paradigms
Is consistent with prevailing values and norms	Conflicts with prevailing values and norms
Can be implemented with existing knowledge and skills	Requires the acquisition of new knowledge and skills
Requires resources and conditions currently available to those responsible for implementing the innovations	Requires resources and conditions not currently available to those responsible for implementing the innovations
Is easily accepted because of common agreement that the innovation is necessary	Is easily resisted because only those who have a broad perspective of the school see the innovation as necessary

Source: Marzano & Kosena, 2022, p. 162. Adapted from Marzano et al., 2005; Marzano & Waters, 2009.

Speaking about implementing both standards-referenced reporting and competency-based education, Robert J. Marzano and Brian J. Kosena (2022) recommended that school leaders ask those who will be implementing the systems the following questions.

- Is the initiative a logical and incremental extension of what we have done in the past?
- Does the initiative fit within the existing paradigms of teachers and administrators?
- Is the initiative consistent with prevailing values and norms?
- Can the initiative be implemented with the knowledge and skills that the faculty and administrators already have?
- Can the initiative be implemented with the resources and conditions that are easily available?
- Is there common agreement that the initiative is necessary? (p. 161)

Robert J. Marzano and Patrick B. Hardy (2023) further explained that "if responses [to the questions] indicate that a majority or even a significant minority of constituents perceive the coming changes as second order" (p. 143), then the leader should not expect buy-in, at least during the initial stages of implementation. In effect, it is legitimate and sometimes necessary for a leader to proceed with an innovation without initial buy-in knowing that they will continue to work on enhancing buy-in over time as appropriate opportunities arise.

Equity

The second reason standards-referenced reporting and CBE are at the top of the framework is that they focus on individual students and, as a result, are naturally oriented toward equity. This is not to say that traditional school structures do not or cannot focus on equity. It is to say, though, that the structural design of standards-referenced reporting and CBE makes such a focus much easier. Since equity is such a voluminous topic, we make a distinction between interactional equity and institutional equity in how we address the subject within the HRS framework.

Interactional Equity

While there are many definitions of equity in the literature, probably the most common definition in general usage is the quality of being fair and impartial (Equity, n.d.). Using this as a starting point, one might make the case that many of the current efforts to enhance equity in K–12 education are focused on what we refer to as *interactional equity*. As its name implies, interactional equity deals with the type of interactions students, teachers, administrators, and staff experience. The basic tenets of equity would require that these interactions should be fair and impartial with all individuals being honored for their uniqueness and no individual being intentionally or unwittingly disrespected by what occurs or does not occur in schools. Interactional equity focuses on people's perceptions and sense of well-being.

It is important to recognize that interactional equity is addressed in levels 1 and 2 of the HRS model. At level 1, the following indicators are designed to ensure that all members of the school community feel that they are recognized and honored for their individuality.

 1.1 The faculty and staff perceive the school environment as safe, supportive, and orderly.

 1.2 Students, parents, and the community perceive the school environment as safe, supportive, and orderly.

These two indicators in particular speak to interactional equity. Many of the programs and practices that schools use to address these indicators include ensuring that all students are treated equitably. Many schools provide training on equitable interactions to staff.

At level 2, the school's instructional model for effective teaching—its "clear vision as to how teachers should address instruction" (indicator 2.1)—can also speak to interactional equity. Although schools implementing the HRS process can use any comprehensive instructional model they so choose (or create their own), we use *The New Art and Science of Teaching* (Marzano, 2017) model as an example. Broadly speaking, this model consists of forty-three elements of effective instruction, ranging from providing scales and rubrics (element 1) to organizing students to interact (element 22) to understanding students' backgrounds and interests (element 39) and many more. The elements are categorized into ten design areas, including using assessments (design area II) and implementing rules and procedures (design area VIII), which are further grouped into three overarching domains: feedback, content, and context. For each element, teachers can choose from a variety of strategies to achieve the desired results. For a complete explanation of the model, refer to *The New Art and Science of Teaching* (Marzano, 2017).

For the purposes of this discussion, it is important to note that many elements in the domain of context—which relates to creating a supportive classroom environment—deal directly with interactional equity. Broadly speaking, interactional equity occurs when the interactions teachers have with students make them feel like they are accepted and honored as individuals, that there is equal opportunity for each student to demonstrate who they are, and for each student to explore who they aspire to be. The following elements address one or more of these characteristics.

- **Element 31:** Providing opportunities for students to talk about themselves—Strategies within this element help ensure that students get to know one another throughout a school.

- **Element 32:** Motivating and inspiring students—Strategies within the element focus on ensuring students have systematic and frequent opportunities to be inspired to become the best versions of themselves.

- **Element 38:** Using verbal and nonverbal behaviors that indicate affection for students—Strategies within this element focus on students receiving continual reinforcement that they are liked.

- **Element 39:** Understanding students' backgrounds and interests—Strategies within this element help teachers become aware of the backgrounds and interests of individuals within the class.

- **Element 40:** Displaying objectivity and control—Strategies within this element help teachers refrain from interacting emotionally with specific students or incidents and instead respond in a way that communicates the teacher is a consistent, supportive partner with students.

- **Element 41:** Demonstrating value and respect for reluctant learners—Strategies within this element help teachers ensure that they focus attention on reluctant learners (that is, those students who seem disenfranchised or shy about participating in the class culture) so they feel as welcome and respected as other students.

- **Element 42:** Asking in-depth questions of reluctant learners—Strategies within this element help teachers ensure that they ask equally challenging questions of reluctant learners so they know that the teacher has high expectations for them.

- **Element 43:** Probing incorrect answers with reluctant learners—Strategies within this element help teachers ensure that they probe the thinking of reluctant learners, particularly when the learner offers a seemingly incorrect answer, to signal to those learners that their logic, while incorrect sometimes, is respected and that making mistakes is a natural part of the learning process.

In addition to communicating an instructional model to teachers, HRS level 2 also includes indicators related to supporting teachers in enhancing their pedagogical skill. Consequently, if a school's instructional model contains elements like those in *The New Art and Science of Teaching* model, then the school is increasing its interactional equity.

Institutional Equity

In contrast to interactional equity, *institutional equity* occurs when the infrastructure of the school does not intentionally or unwittingly pose obstacles to students' learning. At its core, institutional equity deals with opportunity to learn. One approach to addressing institutional equity is Universal Design.

Universal Design originated as a set of principles in the field of architecture. Ron Mace (1985), who established this framework, explained that it is "simply a way of designing a building or facility at little or no extra cost so it is both attractive and functional for all people disabled or not" (p. 147). The original Universal Design principles are as follows (Preiser & Smith, 2011).

1. **Equitable use:** Disabled and able-bodied individuals can use all facilities in the building.
2. **Flexibility in use:** The various facilities of the building can be used in multiple ways.
3. **Simple and intuitive use:** Use of the various facilities in the building is simple and intuitive.
4. **Perceptible information:** Information about how to use the various facilities in the building is in plain sight.
5. **Tolerance for error:** The various facilities in the building allow for people making mistakes when using them without suffering negative consequences.
6. **Low physical effort:** Using the facilities in the building does not require a great deal of physical effort.
7. **Size and space for approach and use:** The size and space for approach and use of facilities should be designed with people with disabilities in mind.

By the beginning of the new millennium, many professions adopted these principles, including education. The principles even made their way into the theory and practice of assessment, as evidenced by their appearance in the 2014 publication of *The Standards for Educational and Psychological Testing*. This publication represents the official position on effective and equitable testing of the American

Educational Research Association, the American Psychological Association, and the National Council on Measurement in Education. One also finds references to Universal Design in many discussions about fairness in educational assessment (Camilli & Newton, 2022). The Universal Design principles certainly can spark new thinking regarding how assessments should be designed and administered in schools. Specifically, consider the following adaptations for assessing students equitably.

1. **Equitable use:** Formats of tests and individual test items do not impede students demonstrating their knowledge of the content.
2. **Flexibility in use:** Assessment information about students should be gathered easily and at virtually any time.
3. **Simple and intuitive use:** Assessments should be transparent in terms of what they are requiring students to do.
4. **Perceptible information:** Not applicable
5. **Tolerance for error:** Educators should distinguish between careless errors and errors that demonstrate a lack of knowledge when assigning students scores on assessments.
6. **Low physical effort:** Students' levels of effort should not be a significant factor in the score students receive.
7. **Size and space for approach and use:** Not applicable

In the context of testing within schools, Universal Design recommendations imply that all students should have access to the same opportunities for assessment, including students with disabilities, English learners, and others who encounter obstacles to fair testing practices. Recommendations to this end include allowing students multiple means of answering test items (orally, in writing, or with assistance from technology, for example) and providing students multiple means to demonstrate what they know (written work, demonstrations, explanations delivered orally, and so on). For detailed descriptions of these and other techniques, see *The New Art and Science of Classroom Assessment* (Marzano et al., 2019).

While the foundational levels of the HRS framework address interactional equity, the more significant structural changes related to standards-referenced reporting and competency-based education help a school directly address institutional equity. We consider standards-referenced reporting (level 4) first.

Standards-Referenced Reporting

Level 4 of the HRS model, standards-referenced reporting, has two indicators:

4.1 The school establishes clear and measurable goals focused on critical needs regarding improving achievement of individual students.

4.2 The school analyzes, interprets, and uses data to regularly monitor progress toward achievement goals for individual students.

Before discussing standards-referenced reporting as second-order change and its application to institutional equity, it's important to take note of the term used for this level. Specifically, this level is referred to as *standards-referenced reporting* as opposed to *standards-based reporting*. This is a very important but often overlooked distinction. Grant Wiggins (1993, 1996) was perhaps the first educator to highlight the differences between a standards-*based* reporting system and a standards-*referenced* system. In a standards-based system, students move to the next level of content when they can demonstrate competence at the current level. Of course, this is the definition of a competency-based system. For all intents and purposes, then, the terms *standards-based* and *competency-based* are synonymous.

Standards-*referenced* reporting, on the other hand, does not require students to demonstrate competency in order to move to the next level. In a standards-referenced system, each student's status is reported relative to each standard or measurement topic addressed during that grading period. In the HRS system, we use measurement topics as opposed to standards because standards are commonly unpacked into multiple topics (as described in big idea 2, page 27). However, even if the student doesn't reach a particular score for each topic, the student moves to the next level at the end of the course or grade level. We have found the vast majority of schools and districts that claim to have standards-based reporting systems in fact have standards-referenced systems.

Standards-referenced reporting has been a part of K–12 education in the United States since before the turn of the millennium. As its name implies, standards-referenced reporting is a by-product of the standards movement, which represented a sea change in education (Marzano & Kendall, 1996). About the standards movement, researchers Robert Glaser and Robert Linn (1993) stated that its significance will only be apparent in retrospect:

> In the recounting of our nation's drive toward educational reform, the last decade of this century will undoubtedly be identified as the time when a concentrated press for national educational standards emerged. The press for standards was evidenced by the efforts of federal and state legislators, presidential and gubernatorial candidates, teachers and subject-matter experts, councils, government agencies, and private foundations. (p. xiii)

Since 2000, a number of efforts have been made to improve on state standards, including the Common Core (NGA & CCSSO, 2010c) and the Next Generation Science Standards (NGSS Lead States, 2013). Educators and researchers have also developed ways to address the persistent issues with standards and make them more actionable in classrooms—for example, through proficiency scales (see big idea 2, page 27). Along the way, it became obvious that standards should also have an effect on traditional methods of grading, such as the omnibus letter grades of A, B, C, D, and F, which have a strong and long-term foothold in U.S. education, particularly at the secondary level (Brookhart et al., 2016).

Over time, the standards-referenced movement has indeed changed grading and reporting practices dramatically. Instead of just an overall grade, it allows teachers to assign students scores on specific measurement topics. This is depicted in figure 5.1. This sample report card is for fourth grade, but the format easily generalizes down to kindergarten and up to grade 12. The primary difference at the high school level would be that the report card is organized by courses as opposed to subject areas at a particular grade level.

To interpret this report card, assume that the school using it is departmentalized at the fourth-grade level. This means that different teachers are responsible for each subject area as opposed to a single teacher in a self-contained classroom being responsible for all subject areas. In the report card, each subject area reports on a number of measurement topics that were taught in class during the grading period. The bar graphs report summative scores on measurement topics. For example, the student in figure 5.1 has a summative score of 2.5 for the measurement topic of Word Recognition and Vocabulary in language arts, and a summative score of 3.0 for the topic of Estimation in mathematics. Of particular interest in this type of report card is that the bar graphs also report growth. The darker part represents the student's

Name:	John Mark	Grade Level:	4
Address:	123 Some Street	Homeroom:	Ms. Smith
City:	Anytown, CO 80000		

Language Arts (LA)	2.46	C	Participation	3.40	A
Mathematics	2.50	B	Work Completion	2.90	B
Science	2.20	C	Behavior	3.40	A
Social Studies	3.10	A	Working in Groups	2.70	B
Art	3.00	A			

		0.5	1.0	1.5	2.0	2.5	3.0	3.5	4.0
LA Reading									
Word Recognition and Vocabulary	2.5								
Reading for Main Idea	1.5								
Literary Analysis	2.0								
LA Writing									
Language Conventions	3.5								
Organization and Focus	2.5								
Research and Technology	1.0								
Evaluation and Revision	2.5								
Writing Applications	3.0								
LA Listening and Speaking									
Comprehension	3.0								
Organization and Delivery	3.0								
Analysis and Evaluation of Oral Media	2.5								
Speaking Applications	2.5								
Life Skills									
Participation	4.0								
Work Completion	3.5								
Behavior	3.5								
Working in Groups	3.0								
Average for Language Arts	2.46								

		0.5	1.0	1.5	2.0	2.5	3.0	3.5	4.0
Mathematics									
Number Systems	3.5								
Estimation	3.0								
Addition/Subtraction	2.5								
Multiplication/Division	2.5								
Ratio/Proportion/Percent	1.0								
Life Skills									
Participation	4.0								
Work Completion	2.0								
Behavior	3.5								
Working in Groups	2.0								
Average for Mathematics	2.50								

Figure 5.1: Standards-referenced report card.

continued ▶

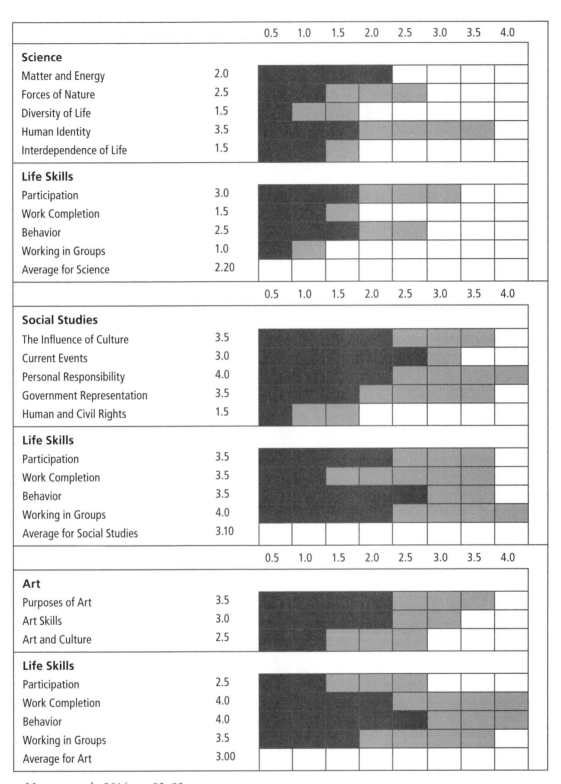

Source: Marzano et al., 2014, pp. 92–93.

status at the beginning of the grading period, and the lighter part represents the student's knowledge gain during the grading period. Finally, the average of the summative scores for the topics in each subject area has been translated to a traditional letter grade, which schools can do if they prefer to also communicate an overall grade.

In addition to making status and growth on specific topics transparent to students and parents, it seems logical that standards-referenced grading practices should be more highly correlated with students' scores on external tests. As a basis for comparison, Susan Brookhart and colleagues (2016) analyzed the research on grading over a one-hundred-year period and found that the correlation between overall grades and students' performance on external tests like a state test is about 0.50. That same analysis, which synthesized research published up to 2014, did *not* find stronger correlations between standards-referenced grades and external test scores.

Since then, however, a number of studies have reported that standards-referenced grading exhibits higher correlations with external tests. For example, Erin Lehman, David De Jong, and Mark Baron (2018) reported the results depicted in table 5.2. The correlations between traditional grades and external tests are substantially lower than the 0.50 reported by Brookhart and colleagues (2016). The correlations between standards-referenced grades and external tests are substantially higher than the correlations involving traditional grades, with two of the three correlations (that is, grades 6 and 8) being substantially higher than the 0.50 criterion.

Table 5.2: Correlation Between Grades and End-of-Year External Assessments

Traditional Grades			Standards-Referenced Grades		
Grade Level	n	Correlation	Grade Level	n	Correlation
6	753	0.348	6	151	0.607
7	595	0.397	7	123	0.465
8	544	0.405	8	103	0.576

Source: © 2018 by International Council of Professors of Educational Administration. Adapted with permission.

Furthermore, studies have examined the correlation between students' standards-referenced scores on proficiency scales as described in this book and their scores on external tests (Haystead & Marzano, 2022; Marzano & Haystead, 2023). Using students' proficiency scale score for mathematics and English language arts and a middle-of-the-year external test, the researchers reported correlations of 0.84 for mathematics and 0.68 for English language arts. In a different study, Cameron L. Rains (2020) reported correlations above 0.90 between elementary students' scores on proficiency scales and their end-of-the-year state tests in mathematics and English language arts.

Standards-referenced grading makes teaching and assessing academic content more equitable in a number of ways, described as follows.

- **Reports status and growth:** Reporting growth implicitly adds a motivational component to grading and reporting. A traditional system only acknowledges and celebrates status, the current level of performance a student can demonstrate. While there is nothing inherently wrong with acknowledging high status each reporting period, the same students tend to achieve those highest levels. It's built into the system. To illustrate, consider the convention of a grade point average (GPA). Again, there is nothing wrong with computing students' GPAs, and this information can be quite useful. However, there are some built-in characteristics that should be acknowledged. Once a student accrues a high GPA for a couple grading periods, that GPA will tend to stay high unless the student exhibits a precipitous drop in letter grades. Again, there is nothing wrong with acknowledging high status; to the contrary, we believe that schools should always acknowledge such accomplishments. But just as high GPAs tend to stay high, it is also the case that low GPAs tend to stay low. This occurs for mathematical reasons, but also because students become discouraged and simply give up. Measuring and reporting growth can alleviate this problem. While a particular student might have relatively low status, they might exhibit high growth during a given grading period. Of course, a number of high-growth grading periods for a particular student will also enhance their overall status.

- **Makes the calculation of overall grades transparent:** As the report card in figure 5.1 (page 73) illustrates, standards-referenced grades explicitly identify what is included in the overall grade. Elements like homework, effort, and adherence to rules can be quantified and included in the overall grade or left out and reported in separate categories. In either case, students and parents have a clear understanding about what contributes to a grade. In contrast, overall grades—not broken into their component parts—give students little if any guidance as to why they received the overall grade and how to improve on it.

- **Allows for student input into the grading process:** One of the biggest boons to equity from standards-referenced grading is that students can interact with the teacher about their grade throughout a grading period. Since they are aware of how the final grade will be constructed, they can advocate for themselves—even suggesting ways they can demonstrate their current status on specific proficiency scales. (For a detailed discussion of these options, consult *The New Art and Science of Classroom Assessment*; Marzano et al., 2019.)

Standards-referenced reporting represents second-order change because it is perceived as a break with the past: it provides summative scores for each student on each topic as opposed to providing only one omnibus score representing all topics assessed. It also conflicts with the prevailing norm that what's included or not included in a student's grade is solely up to the teacher's discretion. Finally, it requires the acquisition of new knowledge and skills, such as how to compute final summative scores for each student on each topic.

Competency-Based Education

The fifth level of the HRS framework is competency-based education. While it is certainly not a new idea, CBE has gained significant traction since 2010 in both K–12 and postsecondary education. For example, in the higher education realm, the U.S. Department of Education announced the Experimental Sites Initiative, also known as the CBE experiment, in July 2014 (Marzano, Norford, Finn, & Finn, 2017). Institutions of higher education were afforded flexibility in using assessments of prior learning to grant credits for content that students had previously mastered. Some institutions developed self-paced competency-based education programs, while others employed a mix of direct assessments and course-work completion. In 2015, the Department of Education expanded the experiment to allow institutions to charge tuition on a subscription basis. This iteration of CBE was designed to allow students to learn as much as possible in the shortest amount of time without paying for additional courses.

The K–12 arena has also seen federal endorsements to develop CBE systems. For example, in 2015, then-secretary of education Arne Duncan praised Purdue University for their CBE programs and suggested its principles should be applied to high schools: "Whether it's an advanced physics class here or engineering, or whether it's algebra as a ninth-grader—if you can demonstrate that you know algebra, why should you sit in that chair for nine months?" (Schneider & Paul, 2015). Secretary Duncan's remarks highlighted a basic premise of competency-based learning: whether it be at the K–12 or college level, learners should be able to move on when they have demonstrated mastery of the content.

In December 2015, Congress reauthorized the Elementary and Secondary Education Act. This legislation, known as the Every Student Succeeds Act, included provisions that directly support competency-based education by allowing K–12 schools to "redesign assessments for student-centered learning, pilot new assessment systems that align with competency-based education approaches, [and] implement personalized, blended, and online learning approaches" (Marzano et al., 2017, p. 5). In response to ESSA, state legislatures and boards of education started bold initiatives to develop and implement CBE systems (Marzano et al., 2017). For example, Tom Torlakson and Michael Kirst (2016) of the California Department of Education proposed "a competency-based system in which schools report student performance relative to competencies rather than traditional grade levels" (Marzano et al., 2017, p. 5). Florida, Georgia, and Idaho enacted similar state initiatives. CompetencyWorks, a collaborative initiative that provides information and knowledge about competency education in the K–12 education system, has systematically tracked state initiatives that promote competency-based approaches and documented dramatic increase in these initiatives between 2012 and 2021 (Weaver, 2023).

While there is agreement that competency-based education approaches are needed in K–12 education, there is not agreement as to the specific components that should comprise an effective CBE system. In deference to this heterogeneity, the HRS framework provides only broad guidelines as to what a school must demonstrate to be certified. Specifically, there are three indicators for level 5.

5.1 Students move on to the next level of the curriculum for any subject area only after they have demonstrated competence at the previous level.

5.2 The school schedule accommodates students moving at a pace appropriate to their situation and needs.

5.3 The school affords students who have demonstrated competency levels greater than those articulated in the system immediate opportunities to begin work on advanced content or career paths of interest.

This level within the HRS framework has the following characteristics that address both interactional and institutional equity.

- **Students move on to the next level of content *only after* they have demonstrated proficiency at the current level:** Some students might take a longer or a much shorter amount of time than is typical to move through the content in a specific subject area at a particular grade level or in a particular course. The implicit message to students is that the structure of the school is committed to their mastering the content. In effect, it represents a vote of confidence that all students can reach high levels of success in the curriculum.

- **Students have multiple opportunities and ways to learn content and demonstrate proficiency:** Structurally, this flexibility increases the chances of students learning content and demonstrating their mastery of the same. In contrast, when a system provides very few specific opportunities or ways to learn content and to demonstrate competence, it inherently discriminates against students who learn in atypical ways and students who know the content but don't do well with traditional testing.

- **Student efficacy and agency are a central focus in addition to proficiency with academic content:** *Efficacy* refers to students' belief that they have some measure of control over the current and future events in their lives. *Agency* is the set of skills that allows efficacy to manifest in students' lives and the opportunities to employ those skills. Intentionally enhancing student efficacy and agency sends a direct message to students that they are respected as unique and powerful individuals.

- **Students have a voice and choices within the teaching and learning process:** *Student voice* means that students are invited to provide input into the teaching and learning process. *Student choice* means that students have options as to the learning and assessment opportunities within a school.

Competency-based education represents second-order change because it alters the traditional notion of grade levels. No longer do students have to wait to receive instruction in specific topics until they reach a specific age or grade level. If students can demonstrate that they are ready to learn new content, they can do so even if that content was traditionally taught at higher grade levels. Additionally, students are not passed from one grade level to the next with major gaps in their knowledge base. Rather, to pass to the next level in a specific content area, students must demonstrate competence in all the content at their current level. CBE also requires the acquisition of new knowledge and skills for teachers, such as how to manage a class of students who are working on different levels of content.

HRS in Practice

Northeast Middle School in Midland, Michigan, made the shift from HRS level 3 to HRS level 4 and implemented proficiency scales as the foundation for standards-referenced reporting. The following personal reflections from Northeast Middle School staff demonstrate the changes in their own practice and the changes they saw in students. Sixth-grade ELA teacher Kelly Brewer offers these comments on the move to using scales and engaging in the HRS level 4 work.

> I'll admit it. At first, I was a skeptic. I was in my twenty-seventh year of teaching when I learned we were moving to the Marzano approach, teaching with proficiency scales as our guide. I had full confidence in the traditional way I had always taught middle school English. Little did I know how much better learning could be. Within one year of using proficiency scales as my guide, my students soared to new heights.
>
> With proficiency scales, the goal is always learning and growth rather than grades. With our scales, students clearly know the endgame—there are no surprises or mysteries. It is a new way of thinking for both teachers and students, and there is a learning curve to be sure, but I can confidently state that in the last five years of teaching with proficiency scales, both the quality and quantity of student output has skyrocketed. I can meet my students where they are, give individualized attention to those who need it, and challenge kids who are ready to extend. Proficiency scales have transformed my thinking about learning in the best way possible.
>
> This approach has also built a real sense of community within my classroom. In our ELA classroom, we are all on the same team, working toward the same goals. The first step: master the score 2.0 vocabulary. We help one another, cheer for one another, and celebrate each student as they achieve their targets. It doesn't matter who finishes first or last, all that matters is we all help one another get there. The proficiency scales are front and center, guiding our learning each day. Students know what is required to achieve success. There are myriad ways to informally assess students to know exactly where they are and

what they need. This allows my feedback to students to be focused and specific, always referencing the scales.

In writing, students can see patterns and trends, pinpoint exactly where they need work, and see a clear path to get there. We read together and have authentic conversations about books, all the while focusing on our proficiency scales; many achieve 3.0 level quite quickly and then extend to amazing heights.

At Northeast, we have three sixth-grade teams with twelve teachers all teaching ELA. Because we teach with proficiency scales, the goals are clear and consistent across classroom, team, and grade. We are all working toward the same goals, which results in focused, productive collaboration. It also provides the ability and freedom to share and group students, both for review and extension, as we all have the same end goals.

Since moving to the use of proficiency scales, we've held student-led conferences, allowing kids to take ownership of their learning; they discuss precisely where they are and where they need to go, all based on the scales. The students are filled with pride, sharing all they've accomplished with their parents. As one student said when debriefing the following day, "I love doing conferences this way. In elementary school, I always felt my parents and teacher were talking behind my back." Exactly. Why would we take students out of the equation? They should be front and center, leading the charge. The scales allow us to accomplish this. (K. Brewer, personal communication, April 9, 2023)

Sarah Wright is an eighth-grade prealgebra teacher at Northeast Middle School and offered her perspective on the use of proficiency scales and how her team developed them from the ground up for the content areas they were teaching.

After teaching at the elementary level for four years, I moved to teaching eighth-grade prealgebra at Northeast Middle School. Northeast was already well established with proficiency scales, but the grade level and content area I was moving into did not have proficiency scales. Over the summer of my grade-level move, I learned all about proficiency scales and the benefits of them. My collaborative team got together and dug into our standards and determined what various levels of proficiency would look like for students with each standard. We designed our first proficiency scales that summer and implemented them that school year. Now in our third year of using our scales, we have adapted them every year and made them better. We can improve them because we have learned more about our standards and our students.

My favorite part of using proficiency scales is my ability to pinpoint exactly what a student must do to improve their grade. With proficiency scales, grades are a better indicator of understanding. When I used traditional grading at the upper elementary level, students who wanted to improve their grade needed to study and work harder to do better on the next assessment. With proficiency scales, students can understand exactly what skills they are lacking evidence for and work to show their understanding of those skills. Proficiency scales allow students to show growth over the whole year and not just within one unit. With proficiency scales, students are encouraged to keep working at skills they are lacking and not just move onto the next unit's skills.

One of my students, who is learning to speak English as a second language, recently came to me and asked what he needed to do to improve his grades. If I were teaching at a school with traditional grading, I would have told him to work hard at our current unit to improve his grade. Instead, we were able to look at his understanding from all units and pinpoint the skills he needed to level up his understanding to the next level of proficiency. He picked one skill to work on for right now. Once this student has practiced and believes he has mastered this skill, he can show me his newly learned skill and improve his grade. Proficiency scales encourage students to never give up on content they did not learn and constantly work on skills they have not yet mastered. (S. Wright, personal communication, April 9, 2023)

Northeast Middle School special education teacher Kerry Limron offers her insights into the individualized approach proficiency scales have brought to the students she serves.

Throughout my whole teaching career, I have never experienced success like I do utilizing proficiency scales. Proficiency scales have totally changed the way that I teach and, more importantly, the way my students learn. For the first time in my career, I know exactly what skills my students are strong in and what skills they need more practice with. When I used the traditional grading system, I never had success like I do now because my students lacked motivation and I did not know exactly what each student needed to grow as a learner.

My [special education] students are very motivated by using the scales and no letter grades. I found that letter grades made my students feel defeated, making them want to give up on learning. Using letter grades was not only demotivating for my students but grades told me nothing about exactly where my students were in their learning process. I have found that using proficiency scales creates classrooms where students are motivated to learn and students are creating their own personal learning goals. Now students have a growth mindset and they try every day to reach a level 3.0 learning goal and beyond. After the exponential growth that I have experienced using proficiency scales, I would never teach any other way. (K. Limron, personal communication, April 9, 2023)

The comments of all three of these teachers put a fine point on the fact that standards-referenced reporting centered around the use of proficiency scales is initially a second-order change for most teachers. They may be skeptical about it, and it challenges their existing paradigms about curriculum, assessment, and instruction. These comments also demonstrate the inherent link to equity. Students feel that what is expected of them is transparent and that the teachers are advocates for their learning as opposed to obstacles.

Standards-referenced reporting can be the desired end point for a school, or it can be a critical step on the road to level 5, CBE. The school John E. Flynn, a Marzano Academy, was the first school in the United States certified at HRS level 5. This K–8 school is in the Westminster Public Schools district outside of Denver, Colorado, which has been a pioneering district in competency-based education since the early 2010s. The first year after the school's 2016 founding, its score on the state's performance framework index was thirty-six points out of a possible one hundred (Kosena & Marzano, 2022). This index is a composite of students' status scores and growth scores on the state test in mathematics and English language arts.

To achieve HRS level 5 status, principal Brian J. Kosena led the staff in adopting the Marzano Academies model, which includes components that address curriculum (including vocabulary and cognitive and metacognitive skills), instruction (including blended instruction and cumulative review), students' experience at school (including inspiration and efficacy and agency), competency-based approaches to assessment, grading, scheduling, and more. The school implemented these components in a staged fashion so that faculty and staff could adequately prepare for the second-order change many of them represented. During their implementation, the principal focused the attention of faculty and staff on the changes and successes of individual students and the fact that the school was implicitly creating a culture in which every student felt welcomed, acknowledged for who they are, and encouraged to become the best version of themselves they could be. The school also provided systematic professional development for all staff on a regular basis. In all, it took about three years to implement their CBE system. By 2019, Flynn's score on the state performance index had risen to 48.4, and by 2022, that score had risen to 70.8 (Kosena & Marzano, 2022). Of course, the interval of time between 2019 and 2022 was the heart of the COVID-19 pandemic, when most schools showed decreases in their scores.

Insights and Actions

One major insight for this big idea is that the ultimate goal of K–12 education should be the success and well-being of each individual student. Schools are not factories turning out widgets where success is measured in terms of the average quality of the widgets. In the factory model, the failure of a few widgets or even a substantial minority of the widgets is acceptable. In schools, the failure of a single student has consequences that ripple into the future—for that student, and likely for the student's family, network, and community. The most common action that stems from this insight is to make structural changes that shift the focus of the school to the success of every individual student as opposed to the average performance of groups of students. This makes the implementation of standards-based reporting or competency-based education two of the most important things a school can do.

Epilogue

The High Reliability Schools framework and the big ideas explored in this book provide schools with the tools to move beyond school reform as measured in terms of average performance and begin conceiving of an effective school as one where every student finds success.

For long-term planning, the five-level hierarchy of the HRS framework provides school leaders a clear picture of what the school's journey will entail through a multiyear period. The continuity created when schools engage in long-term and sustained focus on the initiatives within the five levels of the HRS framework prevents the common pitfall of restarting school improvement efforts each time campus leadership changes. Each level supports and meshes with the prior and subsequent levels, ensuring tight alignment of initiatives over time. The first three levels represent the foundational pieces that need to be in place to address school improvement as a whole school. The top two levels move from focusing on improvement for groups of students to improvement for each individual student.

The HRS process engages three systems-based concepts of data-driven leadership. First, the leading indicators identify the conditions of optimal operation a school wants to establish. The leading indicators tell schools what to think about, not how to think, empowering school leaders to implement systems that meet their unique needs. Second, lagging indicators bring data-driven leadership into focus as the evidence that tells schools their systems are working. Third, quick data safeguard a school's progress by creating an information loop that allows leaders to monitor the health of the systems over time and take action to fix those systems before errors become systemwide failures.

The focus of this book has been on five big ideas that have proven to be important lenses leaders can and should use when implementing the HRS process.

1. Becoming an HRS is a measurement process.
2. Certain levels of the HRS framework have a more direct relationship to student achievement as measured by external tests than others.
3. Schools must tailor programs and practices to their specific needs.
4. Without adequate focus and energy, even effective programs and practices will start to degrade.
5. Standards-referenced reporting and competency-based education are at the top of the HRS framework because of their magnitude of change and their focus on equity.

The first big idea distinguishes the HRS process from an intervention, but the HRS process helps leaders monitor the effectiveness of interventions. The second big idea provides leaders with guidance as to the outcomes they can expect from different levels of the HRS framework, as not all levels of the framework impact student performance in ways that can be directly measured in traditional formats. The third big idea reminds school leaders that the interventions they adopt must commonly be adapted to the local needs and circumstances of their school. The fourth big idea cautions leaders to continuously collect data to ensure that the innovations in the school do not degrade in their effectiveness and to modify or create new procedures when they do. Finally, the fifth big idea provides leaders with guidance as to how they can use standards-referenced grading and competency-based education as tools for equity with the caution that they are both second-order change and must be implemented with that in mind.

The importance of an educated society cannot be overstated. We would argue that it is the cornerstone of democracy in the United States and beyond. Since the inception of the American public school system in the late 1800s, educators have attempted to educate the masses. As society's norms and expectations have changed and grown, educators have likewise increased access to and the quality of the education system. In the 21st century, schools and educators have endeavored to further improve education by building systems that support the success of groups of students. The future of the education system lies in the shift in focus from groups of students to individual students and in building systems that ensure each student's success. The five big ideas of HRS represent a forward-looking vision for schools and educators to continue this transformation of schools.

Appendix

HRS Measurement Tools

This appendix contains a leadership accountability scale, sample lagging indicators, and examples of quick data for each leading indicator in the HRS framework. The leadership accountability scales depict a flow-chart process to guide schools in assessing their current status on each indicator and what the logical next steps will be in the strategic planning process. The sample lagging indicators demonstrate the type of concrete, quantifiable criteria that schools should set for themselves. Finally, we identify multiple ideas for quick data sources schools at the sustaining level can consider collecting to help defeat entropy in their systems. Visit **MarzanoResources.com/reproducibles** for free reproducible versions of these tools.

Level 1

At level 1 of the HRS framework, schools develop a safe, supportive, and collaborative culture.

Leading Indicator 1.1

The faculty and staff perceive the school environment as safe, supportive, and orderly.

Leadership Accountability Scale

Step	Status	Description	Directions
C	4 Sustaining	The school cultivates data through quick data sources to monitor faculty and staff perceptions regarding the safety, supportiveness, and orderliness of the school environment, *and* it takes proper actions to intervene when quick data indicate a potential problem.	If yes, Sustaining If no, Applying
B	3 Applying	The school has developed and implemented well-defined, schoolwide routines and procedures that lead to faculty and staff perceptions of a safe, supportive, and orderly environment, *and* can produce lagging indicator data and concrete artifacts of practice proving the desired effects of these actions.	If yes, go to step C If no, Developing
A	2 Developing	The school has developed and implemented well-defined, schoolwide routines and procedures that lead to faculty and staff perceptions of a safe, supportive, and orderly environment.	If yes, go to step B If no, go to step D
D	1 Beginning	The school is in the beginning, yet incomplete, stages of developing and implementing well-defined schoolwide routines and procedures that lead to faculty and staff perceptions of a safe, supportive, and orderly environment.	If yes, Beginning If no, Not Attempting
	0 Not Attempting	The school has not attempted to develop well-defined schoolwide routines and procedures that lead to faculty and staff perceptions of a safe, supportive, and orderly environment.	

Sample Lagging Indicators and Quick Data

Score	Sample Lagging Indicators With Concrete Criteria and Quantifiable Cut Scores
4 **Sustaining**	In addition to the lagging indicator data for the applying level, school leaders regularly collect and analyze quick data like the following: • Easy-to-collect quantitative opinion data are collected at the conclusion of each threat or emergency drill. • Observation of building safety routines show that 98 percent of staff are abiding by safety protocols. • Periodic focus groups with small groups of staff members are conducted to ascertain the status of staff wellness and to allow leaders to determine additional areas of future support. If the data indicate current or potential problems, school leadership develops and executes plans to address these problems.
3 **Applying**	Written routines and procedures regarding issues such as building security, active threat and emergency response, and staff wellness are in place to guide staff in creating a safe campus environment. Similarly, routines and procedures regarding issues such as student behavior management, restorative discipline, interactional equity practices, and student crisis intervention are in place to guide staff in creating an orderly campus environment. Additionally, staff opinion data are collected regarding the effectiveness of safe and orderly practices and protocols and are analyzed by leaders. Student discipline referral data show a 10 percent (year over year) decrease. Student crisis intervention referral data show a 10 percent (year over year) decrease. 90 percent of teachers report that safe and orderly protocols support their ability to effectively educate their students. 100 percent of staff members report that their wellness is prioritized by leaders.
2 **Developing**	Written routines and procedures exist guiding staff in the creation of a safe campus environment. Written routines and procedures exist guiding the staff in the creation of an orderly campus environment.
1 **Beginning**	Some written routines and procedures are in place to create a safe and orderly campus environment, and some staff members follow the established routines and procedures, even if those protocols are not complete.

Example Quick Data Sources

- Short surveys of staff perceptions regarding safety and orderliness of the school indicate how well the school is living up to its routines and procedures.
- Safety drills are observed and timed to provide data.
- Short teacher surveys reveal perceptions of safety procedures.
- Cumulative or targeted discipline data are reviewed.
- Direct conversations with staff indicate their perceptions on specific aspects of school safety.
- Student behaviors are observed in specific settings, such as the lunchroom or commons areas.

Leading Indicator 1.2

Students, parents, and the community perceive the school environment as safe, supportive, and orderly.

Leadership Accountability Scale

Step	Status	Description	Directions
C	4 Sustaining	The school cultivates data through quick data sources to monitor student, parent, and community perceptions regarding the safety, supportiveness, and orderliness of the school environment, *and* it takes proper actions to intervene when quick data indicate a potential problem.	If yes, Sustaining If no, Applying
B	3 Applying	The school has developed and implemented well-defined, schoolwide routines and procedures that lead to student, parent, and community perceptions of the school environment as safe, supportive, and orderly, *and* can produce lagging indicator data and concrete artifacts of practice proving the desired effects of these actions.	If yes, go to step C If no, Developing
A	2 Developing	The school has developed and implemented well-defined, schoolwide routines and procedures that lead to student, parent, and community perceptions of the school environment as safe, supportive, and orderly.	If yes, go to step B If no, go to step D
D	1 Beginning	The school is in the beginning, yet incomplete, stages of developing and implementing well-defined schoolwide routines and procedures that lead to student, parent, and community perceptions of a safe, supportive, and orderly environment.	If yes, Beginning If no, Not Attempting
	0 Not Attempting	The school has not attempted to develop well-defined schoolwide routines and procedures that lead to student, parent, and community perceptions of a safe, supportive, and orderly environment.	

Sample Lagging Indicators and Quick Data

Score	Sample Lagging Indicators With Concrete Criteria and Quantifiable Cut Scores
4 **Sustaining**	In addition to the lagging indicator data for the applying level, school leaders regularly collect and analyze quick data like the following: • Easy-to-collect quantitative opinion data are collected at the conclusion of each threat or emergency drill. • Observation of building safety routines show that 100 percent of students are abiding by safety protocols. • Periodic focus groups with small groups of students and parents are conducted to ascertain the status of student safety and wellness and to allow leaders to determine additional areas of future support. If the data indicate current or potential problems, school leadership develops and executes plans to address these problems.
3 **Applying**	Students, parents, and the community follow written routines and procedures regarding issues such as building security, active threat and emergency response, traffic and parking, anonymous alert reporting, and student wellness practices. Similarly, routines and procedures regarding issues such as attendance, student behavior management, restorative discipline, and student crisis intervention are followed, creating a safe and orderly campus environment. Additionally, student, parent, and community opinion data are collected regarding the effectiveness of safe and orderly practices and protocols and are analyzed by leaders. 95 percent of parents and the community report that they perceive the school environment to be safe and orderly. Student-to-student discipline-referral (such as bullying, fighting, and so on) data show a 10 percent (year over year) decrease. Student crisis intervention referral data show a 10 percent (year over year) decrease. 95 percent of students report that safe and orderly protocols support their ability to effectively participate in the learning process at school.
2 **Developing**	Written routines and procedures are in place to create a safe and orderly campus environment, and students, parents, and community members follow the established protocols.
1 **Beginning**	Some written routines and procedures are in place to create a safe and orderly campus environment, and some students, parents, and community members follow the established routines and procedures, even if those protocols are not complete.

Example Quick Data Sources

- Short surveys of student and parent perceptions are collected by school leaders to gauge progress.
- Intentional conversations are held with parents and students about specific aspects of the school's operation.
- Students and parents periodically participate in focus groups.
- Student behaviors are observed in specific settings, such as the lunchroom or commons areas.

Leading Indicator 1.3

Teachers have formal roles in the decision-making process regarding school initiatives.

Leadership Accountability Scale

Step	Status	Description	Directions
C	4 Sustaining	The school cultivates data through quick data sources to monitor teachers' formal roles and involvement in decision-making processes, *and* it takes proper actions to intervene when quick data indicate a potential problem.	If yes, Sustaining If no, Applying
B	3 Applying	For specific types of decisions, the school has established formal structures and processes to involve teachers in decision making regarding school initiatives, *and* can provide data and concrete artifacts of practice proving the desired effects of these actions.	If yes, go to step C If no, Developing
A	2 Developing	For specific types of decisions, the school has established formal structures and processes to involve teachers in decision making regarding school initiatives.	If yes, go to step B If no, go to step D
D	1 Beginning	The school is in the beginning, yet incomplete, stages of developing formal structures and processes to involve teachers in decision making regarding school initiatives.	If yes, Beginning If no, Not Attempting
	0 Not Attempting	The school has not attempted to develop formal structures and processes to involve teachers in decision making regarding school initiatives.	

Sample Lagging Indicators and Quick Data

Score	Sample Lagging Indicators With Concrete Criteria and Quantifiable Cut Scores
4 **Sustaining**	In addition to the lagging indicator data for the applying level, school leaders regularly collect and analyze quick data like the following: • Leadership team meeting agendas document that staff members are participating in the decision-making process for school initiatives. • Easy-to-collect quantitative opinion data are collected regarding staff member knowledge of the types of decisions that are made with staff collaboration. • Quick discussions are held with individual staff members regarding their understanding of how staff members participate in the decision-making process for school initiatives. If the data indicate current or potential problems, school leadership develops and executes plans to address these problems.
3 **Applying**	Written protocols are in place to involve the staff in the decision-making process for school initiatives. Written protocols are in place describing the types of school initiatives that staff members are to be involved in. Additionally, the results of the decision-making processes for school initiatives are documented, communicated to all staff, and analyzed by leaders. 98 percent of teachers report understanding the types of decisions they will be involved in making. More than 20 percent of teachers are given the opportunity to participate in the decision-making process regarding school initiatives. 100 percent of the decisions made are documented and shared with the staff.
2 **Developing**	Written protocols are in place to involve the staff in the decision-making process for school initiatives. Written protocols are in place describing the types of school initiatives that staff members are to be involved in.
1 **Beginning**	Some protocols are in place to involve the staff in the decision-making process for school initiatives, or some staff members follow the established protocols, even if those protocols are not complete.

Example Quick Data Sources

• Short surveys are conducted to solicit staff perceptions regarding teacher involvement in decision making.

• Quick conversations with staff members reveal their perceptions of recent decisions regarding school initiatives.

• Quick discussions at staff meetings check on knowledge about recent decisions and how those decisions were made.

• Leadership team members produce short reports on thoughts they have gathered from colleagues about upcoming decisions or recently made decisions.

Leading Indicator 1.4

Teacher teams and collaborative groups regularly interact to address common issues regarding curriculum, assessment, instruction, and the achievement of all students.

Leadership Accountability Scale

Step	Status	Description	Directions
C	4 Sustaining	The school periodically cultivates data through quick data sources to monitor teacher teams and collaborative groups to meet regularly and address issues regarding curriculum, assessment, instruction, and the achievement of all students, *and* it takes proper actions to intervene when quick data indicate a potential problem.	If yes, Sustaining If no, Applying
B	3 Applying	The school has developed formal, schoolwide processes for teacher teams and collaborative groups to meet regularly and address issues regarding curriculum, assessment, instruction, and the achievement of all students, *and* can provide data and concrete artifacts of practice proving the desired effects of these actions.	If yes, go to step C If no, Developing
A	2 Developing	The school has developed formal, schoolwide processes for teacher teams and collaborative groups to meet regularly and address issues regarding curriculum, assessment, instruction, and the achievement of all students.	If yes, go to step B If no, go to step D
D	1 Beginning	The school is in the beginning, yet incomplete, stages of developing formal processes for teacher teams and collaborative groups to meet regularly and address issues regarding curriculum, assessment, instruction, and the achievement of all students.	If yes, Beginning If no, Not Attempting
	0 Not Attempting	The school has not attempted to develop formal processes for teacher teams and collaborative groups to meet regularly and address issues regarding curriculum, assessment, instruction, and the achievement of all students.	

Sample Lagging Indicators and Quick Data

Score	Sample Lagging Indicators With Concrete Criteria and Quantifiable Cut Scores
4 **Sustaining**	In addition to the lagging indicator data for the applying level, school leaders regularly collect and analyze quick data like the following: • Drop-in visits to collaborative team meetings occur to provide leaders with useable data. • Collaborative artifacts, such as copies of common assessments or intervention plans, are collected. • Common assessment data sets are reviewed. • Copies of team agendas or notes from meetings are collected and analyzed. If the data indicate current or potential problems, school leadership develops and executes plans to address these problems.
3 **Applying**	Written protocols are in place to guide collaborative teams regarding how they should operate and what they should produce as a result of their efforts. Additionally, the results of collaborative meetings are documented and regularly collected and analyzed by leaders. At least 90 percent of collaborative teams regularly submit data regarding their results. 100 percent of teachers report that collaborative teams are provided with adequate guidance and feedback.
2 **Developing**	Written protocols are in place for the various decisions collaborative teams should make regarding curriculum, instruction, and assessments. Written protocols are in place for the types of outcomes collaborative teams should monitor regarding their decisions. Written protocols are in place regarding how collaborative teams are to report to school leadership.
1 **Beginning**	Some written protocols are in place to guide collaborative teams, or some collaborative teams follow the established protocols, even if those protocols are not complete.

Example Quick Data Sources

- Drop-in observations are conducted during collaborative team meetings.
- Collaborative artifacts, such as copies of common assessments or intervention plans, are collected.
- Common assessment data sets are reviewed.
- Copies of team agendas or notes from meetings are collected and analyzed.
- Quick discussions are held with individual teachers regarding the current work of their teams.

Leading Indicator 1.5

Teachers and staff have formal ways to provide input regarding the optimal functioning of the school.

Leadership Accountability Scale

Step	Status	Description	Directions
C	4 Sustaining	The school periodically cultivates data through quick data sources to monitor the use of formal processes for teachers and staff to provide input regarding the optimal functioning of the school, *and* it takes proper actions to intervene when quick data indicate a potential problem.	If yes, Sustaining If no, Applying
B	3 Applying	The school has implemented formal processes for teachers and staff to provide input regarding the optimal functioning of the school, *and* can provide data and concrete artifacts of practice proving the desired effects of these actions.	If yes, go to step C If no, Developing
A	2 Developing	The school has implemented formal processes for teachers and staff to provide input regarding the optimal functioning of the school.	If yes, go to step B If no, go to step D
D	1 Beginning	The school is in the beginning, yet incomplete, stages of implementing formal processes for teachers and staff to provide input regarding the optimal functioning of the school.	If yes, Beginning If no, Not Attempting
	0 Not Attempting	The school has not attempted to implement formal processes for teachers and staff to provide input regarding the optimal functioning of the school.	

Sample Lagging Indicators and Quick Data

Score	Sample Lagging Indicators With Concrete Criteria and Quantifiable Cut Scores
4 **Sustaining**	In addition to the lagging indicator data for the applying level, school leaders regularly collect and analyze quick data like the following: • Easy-to-collect quantitative opinion data are collected to determine whether teachers and staff feel that they can provide input regarding optimal school functioning. • Documents capture the input provided by teachers and staff regarding optimal school functioning and are shared. • Agendas from decision-making meetings demonstrate the consideration of teachers and staff input. If the data indicate current or potential problems, school leadership develops and executes plans to address these problems.
3 **Applying**	Teachers and staff provide input regarding optimal school functioning by engaging with processes such as anonymous reporting tools, quarterly written surveys, teacher and staff focus groups, and "ask me anything" teacher visits during contract time. 95 percent of teachers and staff report that they are aware of the scope of processes available for them to provide input regarding optimal school functioning.
2 **Developing**	Formal processes exist and are written that allow teachers and staff to provide input regarding the optimal school functioning.
1 **Beginning**	Some formal processes are in place that allow teachers and staff to provide input regarding the optimal school functioning, even if those processes are not complete.

Example Quick Data Sources

• Usage of formal input sources, such as a digital suggestion link, is monitored.

• When conducting input surveys for staff, the percent of returns is monitored.

• Quick discussions at staff meetings determine staff knowledge of and use of input systems.

Leading Indicator 1.6

Students, parents, and the community have formal ways to provide input regarding the optimal functioning of the school.

Leadership Accountability Scale

Step	Status	Description	Directions
C	4 Sustaining	The school periodically cultivates data through quick data sources to monitor the use of formal processes for students, parents, and the community to provide input regarding the optimal functioning of the school, *and* it takes proper actions to intervene when quick data indicate a potential problem.	If yes, Sustaining If no, Applying
B	3 Applying	The school has implemented formal processes for students, parents, and the community to provide input regarding the optimal functioning of the school, *and* can provide data and concrete artifacts of practice proving the desired effects of these actions.	If yes, go to step C If no, Developing
A	2 Developing	The school has implemented formal processes for students, parents, and the community to provide input regarding the optimal functioning of the school.	If yes, go to step B If no, go to step D
D	1 Beginning	The school is in the beginning, yet incomplete, stages of implementing formal processes for students, parents, and the community to provide input regarding the optimal functioning of the school.	If yes, Beginning If no, Not Attempting
	0 Not Attempting	The school has not attempted to implement formal processes for students, parents, and the community to provide input regarding the optimal functioning of the school.	

Sample Lagging Indicators and Quick Data

Score	Sample Lagging Indicators With Concrete Criteria and Quantifiable Cut Scores
4 **Sustaining**	In addition to the lagging indicator data for the applying level, school leaders regularly collect and analyze quick data like the following: • Easy-to-collect quantitative opinion data are collected to determine whether students, parents, and the community feel that they can provide input regarding optimal school functioning. • Documents capture the input provided by students, parents, and the community regarding optimal school functioning and are shared. • Agendas from decision-making meetings demonstrate the consideration of student, parent, and community input. If the data indicate current or potential problems, school leadership develops and executes plans to address these problems.
3 **Applying**	Students, parents, and the community provide input regarding optimal school functioning by engaging with processes such as anonymous reporting tools, quarterly written surveys, student and parent focus groups, in-person and virtual town hall meetings, leadership visits to parent booster club, or other club or organization meetings. 95 percent of students report that they are aware of the scope of processes available for them to provide input regarding optimal school functioning. 95 percent of parents and the community report that they are aware of the scope of processes available for them to provide input regarding optimal school functioning.
2 **Developing**	Formal processes exist and are written that allow students, parents, and the community to provide input regarding optimal school functioning.
1 **Beginning**	Some processes exist and are written that allow students, parents, and the community to provide input regarding optimal school functioning, even if those processes are not complete.

Example Quick Data Sources

- Usage of formal input sources by students, parents, and community is monitored.
- Quick conversations with students and parents determine their awareness and usage of the input process.

Leading Indicator 1.7

The school acknowledges the success of the whole school as well as individuals within the school.

Leadership Accountability Scale

Step	Status	Description	Directions
C	**4** **Sustaining**	The school periodically cultivates quick data sources to monitor the extent to which people feel acknowledged and celebrated for their contributions, *and* it takes proper actions to intervene when quick data indicate a potential problem.	If yes, Sustaining If no, Applying
B	**3** **Applying**	The school has protocols and practices in place to acknowledge and celebrate the accomplishments of the whole school and individuals within the school, *and* can provide data and concrete artifacts of practice proving the desired effects of these actions.	If yes, go to step C If no, Developing
A	**2** **Developing**	The school has protocols and practices in place to acknowledge and celebrate the accomplishments of the whole school and individuals within the school.	If yes, go to step B If no, go to step D
D	**1** **Beginning**	The school is in the beginning, yet incomplete, stages of implementing protocols and practices to acknowledge and celebrate the accomplishments of the whole school and individuals within the school.	If yes, Beginning If no, Not Attempting
	0 **Not Attempting**	The school has not attempted to implement protocols and practices to acknowledge and celebrate the accomplishments of the whole school and individuals within the school.	

Sample Lagging Indicators and Quick Data

Score	Sample Lagging Indicators With Concrete Criteria and Quantifiable Cut Scores
4 **Sustaining**	In addition to the lagging indicator data for the applying level, school leaders regularly collect and analyze quick data like the following: • In quick conversations with staff, students and parents can explain ways that individual students are acknowledged and celebrated at the school. • Focus groups of teachers can explain ways that individual teachers and teams of teachers are acknowledged and celebrated at the school. • Survey data indicate that students, parents, and staff members can explain ways that the whole school and individuals within the school are acknowledged and celebrated. If the data indicate current or potential problems, school leadership develops and executes plans to address these problems.
3 **Applying**	Protocols and practices are in place to acknowledge and celebrate the accomplishments of the whole school and individuals within the school, such as the use of the school website, social media and other electronic platforms, student and staff of the week or month, teacher-team exemplars and celebrations, positive student communication to parents, student academic and behavior awards, and staff-to-staff affirmations. 90 percent of students report that they feel celebrated and understand the reasons why students are celebrated. 95 percent of teacher teams report that they feel celebrated. 100 percent of school organizations are acknowledged or celebrated throughout the course of a school year.
2 **Developing**	Formal practices and protocols are in place and are written to acknowledge and celebrate the accomplishments of the whole school and individuals within the school.
1 **Beginning**	Some practices and protocols are in place to acknowledge and celebrate the accomplishments of the whole school and individuals within the school, even if those practices and protocols are not complete.

Example Quick Data Sources

- Through quick discussions with students and parents, the school collects data regarding their thoughts about how student success is acknowledged.

- Tracking data indicate the percent of students in the school who are recognized for different accomplishments.

- Tracking data indicate the different groups or organizations that have been acknowledged by the school.

- Clicks on student celebration links on the school web page are counted.

Leading Indicator 1.8

The school manages its fiscal, operational, and technological resources in a way that directly supports teachers.

Leadership Accountability Scale

Step	Status	Description	Directions
C	**4** **Sustaining**	The school periodically cultivates quick data sources to monitor the extent to which its fiscal, operational, and technological resources support teachers, *and* it takes proper actions to intervene when quick data indicate a potential problem.	If yes, Sustaining If no, Applying
B	**3** **Applying**	The school manages its fiscal, operational, and technological resources in a way that directly supports teachers, *and* can provide data and concrete artifacts of practice proving the desired effects of these actions.	If yes, go to step C If no, Developing
A	**2** **Developing**	The school manages its fiscal, operational, and technological resources in a way that directly supports teachers.	If yes, go to step B If no, go to step D
D	**1** **Beginning**	The school is in the beginning, yet incomplete, stages of managing fiscal, operational, and technological resources in a way that supports teachers.	If yes, Beginning If no, Not Attempting
	0 **Not Attempting**	The school has not attempted to manage fiscal, operational, and technological resources in a way that supports teachers.	

Sample Lagging Indicators and Quick Data

Score	Sample Lagging Indicators With Concrete Criteria and Quantifiable Cut Scores
4 **Sustaining**	In addition to the lagging indicator data for the applying level, school leaders regularly collect and analyze quick data like the following: • Budget audits align expenditures to initiatives that support teachers. • In quick conversations, teachers explain that fiscal, operational, and technological resources support them in the classroom. • Survey data indicate that teachers believe that the fiscal, operational, and technological resources support them. If the data indicate current or potential problems, school leadership develops and executes plans to address these problems.
3 **Applying**	Protocols and practices manage fiscal, operational, and technological resources in a way that supports teachers, such as questionnaires that allow teachers to identify specific resources needed to support their teaching practices, professional development in classroom technology available to teachers, and campus operational procedures that protect instructional time. 100 percent of campus budget items support teachers in the classroom. 98 percent of teachers report that instructional time is prioritized and protected. 90 percent of technology budget is spent on instructional technology training or resources.
2 **Developing**	Formal practices and protocols are in place and are written that manage fiscal, operational, and technological resources in a way that supports teachers.
1 **Beginning**	Some practices and protocols are in place that manage fiscal, operational, and technological resources in a way that supports teachers, even if those practices and protocols are not complete.

Example Quick Data Sources

- Department chairs or grade-level leaders hold discussions with staff to determine resources they have or need.
- Exit tickets distributed after staff meetings ask teachers about resource needs.
- Data tracking indicates the percent of requests for resources that have been supplied.

Level 2

At level 2 of the HRS framework, schools develop effective teaching in every classroom.

Leading Indicator 2.1

The school communicates a clear vision as to how teachers should address instruction.

Leadership Accountability Scale

Step	Status	Description	Directions
C	4 Sustaining	The school cultivates information through quick data sources to monitor the extent to which the schoolwide language or model of instruction is consistently used, *and* it takes proper actions to intervene when quick data indicate a potential problem.	If yes, Sustaining If no, Applying
B	3 Applying	The school has implemented a schoolwide language or model of instruction, *and* can produce lagging indicator data and concrete artifacts of practice to show the model of instruction is being used in classrooms.	If yes, go to step C If no, Developing
A	2 Developing	The school has implemented a schoolwide language or model of instruction.	If yes, go to step B If no, go to step D
D	1 Beginning	The school is in the beginning, yet incomplete, stages of implementing a schoolwide language or model of instruction.	If yes, Beginning If no, Not Attempting
	0 Not Attempting	The school has not attempted to implement a schoolwide language or model of instruction.	

Sample Lagging Indicators and Quick Data

Score	Sample Lagging Indicators With Concrete Criteria and Quantifiable Cut Scores
4 **Sustaining**	In addition to the lagging indicator data for the applying level, school leaders regularly collect and analyze quick data like the following: • Student surveys indicate teachers use specific classroom practices from the school's instructional model. • In quick conversations, teachers can reference specific areas of instruction they use from the school's instructional model. • Walkthrough observation data clearly reflect practices from the school's instructional model. If the data indicate current or potential problems, school leadership develops and executes plans to address these problems.
3 **Applying**	The school has a written document in place that articulates the schoolwide model of instruction. The school provides professional development opportunities for new teachers regarding the schoolwide model of instruction. Walkthrough observation data reflect practices from the school's instructional model 95 percent of the time. When asked, 100 percent of teachers can reference specific areas of instruction they use from the school's instructional model.
2 **Developing**	The school has a written document in place that articulates the schoolwide model of instruction.
1 **Beginning**	Some practices are in place that articulate the schoolwide model of instruction, even if those practices and protocols are not complete.

Example Quick Data Sources

- Walkthrough observation cumulative data indicate schoolwide use of instructional model practices.

- Randomly collected artifacts of instructional practice clearly indicate the use of practices within the school's instructional model.

- When asked about practices being used in the classroom, teachers speak with the common language of the instructional model used by the school.

- When asked about activities in class, student answers clearly indicate practices from the school's instructional model.

- Elements identified as daily practices in the school's instructional model are evident in 100 percent of classrooms during random walkthrough observations.

Leading Indicator 2.2

The school supports teachers to continually enhance their pedagogical skills through reflection and professional growth plans.

Leadership Accountability Scale

Step	Status	Description	Directions
C	4 Sustaining	The school cultivates information through quick data sources to monitor the extent to which all teachers establish growth goals for pedagogical skills and track their individual progress, *and* it takes proper actions to intervene when quick data indicate a potential problem.	If yes, Sustaining If no, Applying
B	3 Applying	The school has protocols and practices in place to ensure that all teachers establish growth goals for pedagogical skills and track their individual progress, *and* can produce lagging indicator data and concrete artifacts of practice proving the desired effects of these actions.	If yes, go to step C If no, Developing
A	2 Developing	The school has protocols and practices in place to ensure that all teachers establish growth goals for pedagogical skills and track their individual progress.	If yes, go to step B If no, go to step D
D	1 Beginning	The school is in the beginning, yet incomplete, stages of drafting protocols and practices to ensure that all teachers establish growth goals for pedagogical skills and track their individual progress.	If yes, Beginning If no, Not Attempting
	0 Not Attempting	The school has not attempted to ensure that all teachers establish growth goals for pedagogical skills and track their individual progress.	

Sample Lagging Indicators and Quick Data

Score	Sample Lagging Indicators With Concrete Criteria and Quantifiable Cut Scores
4 **Sustaining**	In addition to the lagging indicator data for the applying level, school leaders regularly collect and analyze quick data like the following: • In quick conversations, teachers can identify their specific pedagogical growth goals. • Periodic observation of teachers' individual goal tracking shows progress in effectiveness of the specific pedagogical skill. If the data indicate current or potential problems, school leadership develops and executes plans to address these problems.
3 **Applying**	Protocols and practices are in place to ensure that teachers establish growth goals for pedagogical skills and track their individual progress. 100 percent of teachers have established pedagogical growth goals aligned with the schoolwide model of instruction. Teachers review their growth goals, self-rate, and track their individual progress at least once per quarter. 50 percent of each individual teacher's classroom observation feedback is specific to their individual growth goals. 100 percent of teachers report annual improvement to their pedagogical skills specific to their identified growth goals.
2 **Developing**	Formal protocols and practices are in place to ensure that teachers establish growth goals for pedagogical skills and track their individual progress.
1 **Beginning**	Some protocols and practices are in place to ensure that teachers establish growth goals for pedagogical skills and track their individual progress, even if those practices and protocols are not complete.

Example Quick Data Sources

- Teachers have tracking documents to show their growth in a specific aspect of instruction.
- When asked about their goal progress, teachers can give specific examples of how they have grown in their goal area.
- Digital portfolios show examples of practice within each teacher's goal area.
- Periodic schoolwide tracking of growth-goal progress indicates 90 percent or more of teachers are showing growth in their pedagogical goal areas.

Leading Indicator 2.3

The school is aware of and monitors predominant instructional practices.

Leadership Accountability Scale

Step	Status	Description	Directions
C	4 Sustaining	The school cultivates information through quick data sources to monitor predominant schoolwide instructional practices, *and* it takes proper actions to intervene when quick data indicate a potential problem.	If yes, Sustaining If no, Applying
B	3 Applying	The school has protocols and practices in place to monitor the predominant schoolwide instructional practices, *and* can provide data and concrete artifacts of practice proving the desired effects of these actions.	If yes, go to step C If no, Developing
A	2 Developing	The school has protocols and practices in place to monitor the predominant schoolwide instructional practices.	If yes, go to step B If no, go to step D
D	1 Beginning	The school is in the beginning, yet incomplete, stages of drafting protocols and practices for monitoring the predominant schoolwide instructional practices.	If yes, Beginning If no, Not Attempting
	0 Not Attempting	The school has not attempted to monitor the predominant schoolwide instructional practices.	

Sample Lagging Indicators and Quick Data

Score	Sample Lagging Indicators With Concrete Criteria and Quantifiable Cut Scores
4 **Sustaining**	In addition to the lagging indicator data for the applying level, school leaders regularly collect and analyze quick data like the following: • The use of focused walkthrough visits shows patterns of evidence that specific instructional practices are manifesting in classrooms. • In quick conversations, teachers can explain the schoolwide predominant practices. • Quick data are collected that demonstrate the presence of specific predominant instructional practices at various points throughout the school year. If the data indicate current or potential problems, school leadership develops and executes plans to address these problems.
3 **Applying**	Protocols and practices are in place to monitor the predominant schoolwide instructional strategies. 98 percent of teachers know the predominant schoolwide instructional strategies. 100 percent of classroom observations are tracked and indicate the presence or absence of instructional practices aligned to the school's instructional model. 90 percent of teacher professional development is informed by aggregated predominant-practice classroom walkthrough data. Meeting agendas and internal communication documents indicate that school leaders share the predominant-practice information with their staff.
2 **Developing**	Formal protocols and practices are in place to monitor the predominant schoolwide instructional strategies.
1 **Beginning**	Some protocols and practices are in place to monitor the predominant schoolwide instructional strategies, even if those practices and protocols are not complete.

Example Quick Data Sources

- Quick surveys of teachers show clear predominant practices being used schoolwide. (Example: A one-question survey asking teachers about a successful instructional activity they have recently used indicates a schoolwide use of student vocabulary journals.)

- Quick conversations with students about instructional activities they have been engaged in during their classes show a clear pattern of schoolwide practices.

- Quick discussions at staff meetings asking for specific examples of practices used recently indicate clear schoolwide predominant practices.

- Deliberate, schoolwide focus on instructional elements is easily seen and heard during random walkthroughs.

Leading Indicator 2.4

The school provides teachers with clear, ongoing evaluations of their pedagogical strengths and weaknesses that are based on multiple sources of data and consistent with student achievement data.

Leadership Accountability Scale

Step	Status	Description	Directions
C	4 Sustaining	The school cultivates information through quick data gathered from multiple sources to monitor the collection of specific evaluation data for each teacher regarding pedagogical strengths and weaknesses, *and* it takes proper actions to intervene when quick data indicate a potential problem.	If yes, Sustaining If no, Applying
B	3 Applying	The school has protocols and practices in place to ensure that specific evaluation data gathered from multiple sources are collected for each teacher regarding pedagogical strengths and weaknesses, *and* can provide data and concrete artifacts of practice proving the desired effects of these actions.	If yes, go to step C If no, Developing
A	2 Developing	The school has protocols and practices in place to ensure that specific evaluation data are collected for each teacher regarding pedagogical strengths and weaknesses and that these data are gathered from multiple sources.	If yes, go to step B If no, go to step D
D	1 Beginning	The school is in the beginning, yet incomplete, stages of drafting protocols and practices to ensure that specific evaluation data are collected for each teacher regarding pedagogical strengths and weaknesses and that these data are gathered from multiple sources.	If yes, Beginning If no, Not Attempting
	0 Not Attempting	The school has not attempted to ensure that specific evaluation data are collected for each teacher regarding pedagogical strengths and weaknesses and that these data are gathered from multiple sources.	

Sample Lagging Indicators and Quick Data

Score	Sample Lagging Indicators With Concrete Criteria and Quantifiable Cut Scores
4 **Sustaining**	In addition to the lagging indicator data for the applying level, school leaders regularly collect and analyze quick data like the following: • In quick conversations, teachers can describe their most recent teacher evaluation data. • Quick comparisons between teacher evaluation data and their student achievement data show a positive correlation. • In quick conversations, administrators can explain the various types of data they use to conduct teacher evaluation. If the data indicate current or potential problems, school leadership develops and executes plans to address these problems.
3 **Applying**	Protocols and practices are in place to ensure that specific evaluation data are collected for each teacher regarding pedagogical strengths and weaknesses and that these data are gathered from multiple sources. The administration sorts teachers into tiers based on evaluated strengths and weaknesses, providing differentiated support and monitoring with clear quantitative goals to adjust teachers' tier level at specific points throughout the school year. 100 percent of teacher evaluations are based on multiple sources of information, including direct observation, teacher self-reports, and student achievement data. 100 percent of teachers are observed and given feedback at least once per semester.
2 **Developing**	Formal protocols and practices are in place to ensure that specific evaluation data are collected for each teacher regarding pedagogical strengths and weaknesses and that these data are gathered from multiple sources.
1 **Beginning**	Some protocols and practices are in place to ensure that specific evaluation data are collected for each teacher regarding pedagogical strengths and weaknesses and that these data are gathered from multiple sources, even if those practices and protocols are not complete.

Example Quick Data Sources

- Non-observational evidence and artifacts supplied by teachers provide additional evidence and data regarding teacher effectiveness in specific instructional areas.

- Tracking documents, such as spreadsheets or calendars, indicate periodic classroom observations other than formal, scheduled observations.

- When asked, teachers can provide examples of feedback they have received and put into practice through the observation and evaluation process.

Leading Indicator 2.5

The school provides teachers with job-embedded professional development that is directly related to their instructional growth goals.

Leadership Accountability Scale

Step	Status	Description	Directions
C	4 Sustaining	The school cultivates data through quick data sources to monitor job-embedded professional development directly related to teachers' instructional growth goals, *and* it takes proper actions to intervene when quick data indicate a potential problem.	If yes, Sustaining If no, Applying
B	3 Applying	The school has protocols and practices in place to ensure that job-embedded professional development directly related to teachers' instructional growth goals is provided, *and* can provide data and concrete artifacts of practice proving the desired effects of these actions.	If yes, go to step C If no, Developing
A	2 Developing	The school has protocols and practices in place to ensure that job-embedded professional development directly related to teachers' instructional growth goals is provided.	If yes, go to step B If no, go to step D
D	1 Beginning	The school is in the beginning, yet incomplete, stages of drafting protocols and practices to ensure that job-embedded professional development directly related to teachers' instructional growth goals is provided.	If yes, Beginning If no, Not Attempting
	0 Not Attempting	The school has not attempted to ensure that job-embedded professional development directly related to teachers' instructional growth goals is provided.	

Sample Lagging Indicators and Quick Data

Score	Sample Lagging Indicators With Concrete Criteria and Quantifiable Cut Scores
4 **Sustaining**	In addition to the lagging indicator data for the applying level, school leaders regularly collect and analyze quick data like the following: • Survey data indicate that teachers can describe specific practices they are trying because of job-embedded professional development. • In quick conversations, teachers can explain how job-embedded professional development supports their progress regarding their instructional growth goals. • Periodic focus groups with small groups of teachers are conducted to ascertain the status of job-embedded professional development practices to allow leaders to determine additional areas of future support. If the data indicate current or potential problems, school leadership develops and executes plans to address these problems.
3 **Applying**	Protocols and practices are in place to ensure that job-embedded professional development directly related to teachers' instructional growth goals is provided. 50 percent of professional development is developed to allow teachers access to resources regarding their individual growth goals. 90 percent of teachers video record their own instruction and reflect upon their instructional growth goals with a colleague, instructional coach, or administrator. 95 percent of teachers attend teacher-led professional development specific to their instructional growth goals. 100 percent of teachers have instructional coaching available to them regarding their instructional growth goals.
2 **Developing**	Formal protocols and practices are in place to ensure that job-embedded professional development directly related to teachers' instructional growth goals is provided.
1 **Beginning**	Some protocols and practices are in place to ensure that job-embedded professional development directly related to teachers' instructional growth goals is provided, even if those practices and protocols are not complete.

Example Quick Data Sources

- Instructional coaching documents clearly show teachers are provided with the opportunities for instructional coaching focused on their growth-goal areas.
- Professional development rosters or sign-up sheets indicate matches between professional development sessions and teachers' growth-goal areas.
- Reflection forms indicate teachers have engaged in self-observation of their goal area using video.
- Personal, professional development plans show alignment of professional development activities and teachers' growth-goal areas.

Leading Indicator 2.6

Teachers have opportunities to observe and discuss effective teaching.

Leadership Accountability Scale

Step	Status	Description	Directions
C	4 Sustaining	The school cultivates data through quick data sources to monitor teachers' opportunities to observe and discuss effective teaching virtually or in person, *and* it takes proper actions to intervene when quick data indicate a potential problem.	If yes, Sustaining If no, Applying
B	3 Applying	The school has protocols and practices in place to ensure that teachers have opportunities to observe and discuss effective teaching virtually or in person, *and* can provide data and concrete artifacts of practice proving the desired effects of these actions.	If yes, go to step C If no, Developing
A	2 Developing	The school has protocols and practices in place to ensure that teachers have opportunities to observe and discuss effective teaching virtually or in person.	If yes, go to step B If no, go to step D
D	1 Beginning	The school is in the beginning, yet incomplete, stages of implementing protocols and practices to ensure that teachers have opportunities to observe and discuss effective teaching virtually or in person.	If yes, Beginning If no, Not Attempting
	0 Not Attempting	The school has not attempted to ensure that teachers have opportunities to observe and discuss effective teaching virtually or in person.	

Sample Lagging Indicators and Quick Data

Score	Sample Lagging Indicators With Concrete Criteria and Quantifiable Cut Scores
4 **Sustaining**	In addition to the lagging indicator data for the applying level, school leaders regularly collect and analyze quick data like the following: • Easy-to-collect opinion data are collected to capture positive aspects of and areas for potential future improvement of instructional rounds. • In quick conversations, teachers can explain how instructional rounds support their progress regarding their instructional growth goals. • Documents from instructional rounds summarize teacher discussion and key learning points. If the data indicate current or potential problems, school leadership develops and executes plans to address these problems.
3 **Applying**	Protocols and practices are in place to ensure that teachers have opportunities to observe and discuss effective teaching virtually or in person. 100 percent of teachers participate in instructional rounds at least once per year. 100 percent of teachers have access to view video or virtual examples of exemplary instruction. 40 percent of teacher collaborative planning time is dedicated to discussing effective instructional practices.
2 **Developing**	Formal protocols and practices are in place to ensure that teachers have opportunities to observe and discuss effective teaching virtually or in person.
1 **Beginning**	Some protocols and practices are in place to ensure that teachers have opportunities to observe and discuss effective teaching virtually or in person, even if those practices and protocols are not complete.

Example Quick Data Sources

- Sign-up forms indicate the percentage of teachers who have participated in at least one instructional round session.
- Reflection forms show important discussion points after teachers have observed instructional practices in person or virtually.
- Exit-survey responses indicate practice ideas teachers will try.
- Quick observations show teachers are participating in, observing, and discussing effective teaching sessions.
- Calendars indicate the specific dates that instructional rounds have taken place and the number of teachers who participated.

Level 3

At level 3 of the HRS framework, schools develop a guaranteed and viable curriculum.

Leading Indicator 3.1

The school curriculum and accompanying assessments adhere to state and district standards.

Leadership Accountability Scale

Step	Status	Description	Directions
C	4 Sustaining	The school cultivates information, through quick data sources, to monitor the extent to which the schoolwide protocols and practices in place ensure that the school's curriculum and accompanying assessments adhere to state and district standards, *and* it takes proper actions to intervene when quick data indicate a potential problem.	If yes, Sustaining If no, Applying
B	3 Applying	The school has protocols and practices in place to ensure that the school's curriculum and accompanying assessments adhere to state and district standards, *and* can produce lagging indicator data and concrete artifacts of practice proving the desired effects of these actions.	If yes, go to step C If no, Developing
A	2 Developing	The school has protocols and practices in place to ensure that the school's curriculum and accompanying assessments adhere to state and district standards.	If yes, go to step B If no, go to step D
D	1 Beginning	The school is in the beginning, yet incomplete, stages of implementing protocols and practices to ensure that the school's curriculum and accompanying assessments adhere to state and district standards.	If yes, Beginning If no, Not Attempting
	0 Not Attempting	The school has not attempted to implement protocols and practices to ensure that the school's curriculum and accompanying assessments adhere to state and district standards.	

Sample Lagging Indicators and Quick Data

Score	Sample Lagging Indicators With Concrete Criteria and Quantifiable Cut Scores
4 **Sustaining**	In addition to the lagging indicator data for the applying level, school leaders regularly collect and analyze quick data like the following: • The administration reviews collaborative team curriculum and assessment documents and provides feedback to teams quarterly. • During classroom observations, alignment between instruction, assessment, and priority standards is evident. • In quick conversations, teachers can identify specific standards they address when unit and lesson planning. If the data indicate current or potential problems, school leadership develops and executes plans to address these problems.
3 **Applying**	Protocols and practices are in place to ensure that the school's curriculum and accompanying assessments adhere to state and district standards. 100 percent of collaborative teams develop and submit scope-and-sequence documents, indicating which standards they will prioritize teaching, in which order, and when. 100 percent of collaborative teams plan with curriculum documents that correlate with state and district standards. 100 percent of classroom assessments are aligned to the identified priority standards.
2 **Developing**	Formal practices and protocols are in place to ensure that the school's curriculum and accompanying assessments adhere to state and district standards.
1 **Beginning**	Some practices and protocols are in place to ensure that the school's curriculum and accompanying assessments adhere to state and district standards, even if those practices and protocols are not complete.

Example Quick Data Sources

- Walkthrough observation data indicate instruction is being planned with the guaranteed and viable curriculum in mind.
- Randomly collected classroom assessments indicate the guaranteed and viable curriculum is being assessed.
- When asked, teachers can identify the standards they are currently addressing.
- When asked, students are aware of the specific knowledge they are being asked to learn, and that knowledge reflects the school's curriculum.
- Observations of professional learning community team meetings clearly indicate the team is using the school's curriculum to guide team collaboration.

Leading Indicator 3.2

The school curriculum is focused enough that teachers can adequately address it in the time they have available.

Leadership Accountability Scale

Step	Status	Description	Directions
C	4 Sustaining	The school cultivates information through quick data sources to monitor the extent to which the curriculum for all content areas is focused enough that teachers can adequately address it in the time available, *and* it takes proper actions to intervene when quick data indicate a potential problem.	If yes, Sustaining If no, Applying
B	3 Applying	The school has protocols and practices in place to ensure that the curriculum for all content areas is focused enough that teachers can adequately address it in the time available, *and* can produce lagging indicator data and concrete artifacts of practice proving the desired effects of these actions.	If yes, go to step C If no, Developing
A	2 Developing	The school has protocols and practices in place to ensure that the curriculum for all content areas is focused enough that teachers can adequately address it in the time available.	If yes, go to step B If no, go to step D
D	1 Beginning	The school is in the beginning, yet incomplete, stages of ensuring that the curriculum for all content areas is focused enough that teachers can adequately address it in the time available.	If yes, Beginning If no, Not Attempting
	0 Not Attempting	The school has not attempted to ensure the curriculum for all content areas is focused enough that teachers can adequately address it in the time available.	

Sample Lagging Indicators and Quick Data

Score	Sample Lagging Indicators With Concrete Criteria and Quantifiable Cut Scores
4 **Sustaining**	In addition to the lagging indicator data for the applying level, school leaders regularly collect and analyze quick data like the following: • In quick conversations, teachers explain that they feel that they can adequately address the curriculum in the time they have available. • Survey data indicate that teachers believe that they can adequately address the curriculum in the time they have available. • Periodic reviews of collaborative team meeting notes and documents indicate teachers have adequate time to teach the identified priority standards. If the data indicate current or potential problems, school leadership develops and executes plans to address these problems.
3 **Applying**	Protocols and practices are in place to ensure that the curriculum for all content areas is focused enough that teachers can adequately address it in the time available. 90 percent of teachers explain that they have the time necessary to teach the priority standards during the school day and throughout the school year. 100 percent of classes or courses taught can produce documents identifying the identified priority standards. 90 percent of students explain that they have enough time to learn the content presented to them by their teachers.
2 **Developing**	Formal practices and protocols are in place to ensure that the curriculum for all content areas is focused enough that teachers can adequately address it in the time available.
1 **Beginning**	Some practices and protocols are in place to ensure that the curriculum for all content areas is focused enough that teachers can adequately address it in the time available, even if those practices and protocols are not complete.

Example Quick Data Sources

- When asked, teachers indicate that instructional pacing documents allow adequate time for high-quality instruction to occur.
- Discussion with teachers indicates they know they can add instructional days for topics as necessary.
- Collaborative team artifacts and discussions show that teams make decisions to invest additional time as needed for specific topics they are teaching.
- Surveys of teachers or teacher teams indicate they have adequate time to address the curriculum they are asked to teach.

Leading Indicator 3.3

All students have the opportunity to learn the critical content of the curriculum.

Leadership Accountability Scale

Step	Status	Description	Directions
C	**4** **Sustaining**	The school cultivates information through quick data sources to monitor that all courses and classes directly address the priority standards or topics in the school's curriculum, making sure all students have access to critical content, *and* it takes proper actions to intervene when quick data indicate a potential problem.	If yes, Sustaining If no, Applying
B	**3** **Applying**	The school has protocols and practices in place to ensure that all courses and classes directly address the priority standards or topics in the school's curriculum, making sure all students have access to critical content, *and* can provide data and concrete artifacts of practice proving the desired effects of these actions.	If yes, go to step C If no, Developing
A	**2** **Developing**	The school has protocols and practices in place to ensure that all courses and classes directly address the priority standards or topics in the school's curriculum, making sure all students have access to critical content.	If yes, go to step B If no, go to step D
D	**1** **Beginning**	The school is in the beginning, yet incomplete, stages of ensuring that all courses and classes directly address the priority standards or topics in the school's curriculum, making sure all students have access to critical content.	If yes, Beginning If no, Not Attempting
	0 **Not Attempting**	The school has not attempted to ensure that all courses and classes directly address the priority standards or topics in the school's curriculum, making sure all students have access to critical content.	

Sample Lagging Indicators and Quick Data

Score	Sample Lagging Indicators With Concrete Criteria and Quantifiable Cut Scores
4 **Sustaining**	In addition to the lagging indicator data for the applying level, school leaders regularly collect and analyze quick data like the following: • The administration reviews collaborative team curriculum and assessment documents and provides feedback to teams quarterly. • Collaborative team meetings and classroom observations indicate that all teachers on the team address the priority standards at the same time. If the data indicate current or potential problems, school leadership develops and executes plans to address these problems.
3 **Applying**	Protocols and practices are in place to ensure that all courses and classes directly address the priority standards or topics in the school's curriculum, making sure all students have access to critical content. 100 percent of classes or courses have documents identifying the priority standards, key content vocabulary, and metacognitive skills to be directly taught. 100 percent of classes or courses publish documents identifying priority standards, key content vocabulary, and metacognitive skills, making that information transparent for students, parents, and staff. 100 percent of teachers who teach the same course address the priority standards within their unit and daily planning.
2 **Developing**	Formal practices and protocols are in place to ensure that all courses and classes directly address the priority standards or topics in the school's curriculum, making sure all students have access to critical content.
1 **Beginning**	Some practices and protocols are in place to ensure that all courses and classes directly address the priority standards or topics in the school's curriculum, making sure all students have access to critical content, even if those practices and protocols are not complete.

Example Quick Data Sources

- Common assessment data are available to show progress for groups of learners.
- Conversations with teachers indicate the use of the school's curriculum by each teacher who teaches a common grade or course.
- Observation data indicate teachers of like content are using the school's curriculum.
- Observation or artifacts of collaborative team practices clearly indicate all teachers are addressing the school's curriculum.
- Intervention data show students who need additional opportunities to learn the content are being given that opportunity.

Leading Indicator 3.4

The school establishes clear and measurable goals that are focused on critical needs regarding improving overall student achievement at the school level.

Leadership Accountability Scale

Step	Status	Description	Directions
C	4 Sustaining	The school cultivates information through quick data sources to monitor progress toward schoolwide student achievement goals, *and* it takes proper actions to intervene when quick data indicate a potential problem.	If yes, Sustaining If no, Applying
B	3 Applying	The school has established clear and measurable goals with specific timelines focused on critical needs regarding improving student achievement at the school level, *and* can provide student achievement data measured by an external assessment to show those goals have been attained.	If yes, go to step C If no, Developing
A	2 Developing	The school has established clear and measurable goals with specific timelines focused on critical needs regarding improving student achievement at the school level.	If yes, go to step B If no, go to step D
D	1 Beginning	The school is in the beginning, yet incomplete, stages of establishing clear and measurable goals with specific timelines focused on critical needs regarding improving student achievement at the school level.	If yes, Beginning If no, Not Attempting
	0 Not Attempting	The school has not attempted to ensure that it has clear and measurable goals with specific timelines focused on critical needs regarding improving student achievement at the school level.	

Sample Lagging Indicators and Quick Data

Score	Sample Lagging Indicators With Concrete Criteria and Quantifiable Cut Scores
4 **Sustaining**	In addition to the lagging indicator data for the applying level, school leaders regularly collect and analyze quick data like the following: • The administration reviews student achievement progress toward team SMART (strategic and specific, measurable, attainable, results oriented, time bound) goals quarterly. • Observations of collaborative team meetings indicate that teachers are aware of and using student achievement progress toward SMART goals to make future instructional and intervention decisions. • In quick conversations, teachers can describe their team's progress toward their SMART goals. If the data indicate current or potential problems, school leadership develops and executes plans to address these problems.
3 **Applying**	Clear and measurable goals with specific timelines focused on critical needs regarding improving student achievement at the school level are established. 100 percent of collaborative teams have set and posted SMART goals for student achievement for each priority standard or topic in their course. 100 percent of individual teachers and teacher teams have established written goals as a percentage of students who will score at a proficient level or higher on benchmark and state assessments. 100 percent of individual teachers and teacher teams have established written goals for eliminating differences in achievement for students of different socioeconomic levels, different learning needs, or differing ethnicities.
2 **Developing**	Clear and measurable goals are established with specific timelines focused on critical needs regarding improving student achievement at the school level.
1 **Beginning**	Some goals are established with specific timelines focused on critical needs regarding improving student achievement at the school level, even if those goals are not clear and measurable.

Example Quick Data Sources

- Collaborative teams or individual teachers set short-term SMART goals that align with schoolwide achievement goals.
- When asked, teachers can identify the schoolwide achievement goals.

Leading Indicator 3.5

The school analyzes, interprets, and uses data to regularly monitor progress toward school achievement goals.

Leadership Accountability Scale

Step	Status	Description	Directions
C	**4** **Sustaining**	The school cultivates data through quick data sources to monitor the use of systems and practices for monitoring progress toward school achievement goals, *and* it takes proper actions to intervene when quick data indicate a potential problem.	If yes, Sustaining If no, Applying
B	**3** **Applying**	The school has established systems and practices for monitoring progress toward school achievement goals, *and* can provide data and concrete artifacts of practice proving the desired effects of these actions.	If yes, go to step C If no, Developing
A	**2** **Developing**	The school has established systems and practices for monitoring progress toward school achievement goals.	If yes, go to step B If no, go to step D
D	**1** **Beginning**	The school is in the beginning, yet incomplete, stages of establishing systems and practices for monitoring progress toward school achievement goals.	If yes, Beginning If no, Not Attempting
	0 **Not Attempting**	The school has not attempted to establish systems and practices for monitoring progress toward school achievement goals.	

Sample Lagging Indicators and Quick Data

Score	Sample Lagging Indicators With Concrete Criteria and Quantifiable Cut Scores
4 **Sustaining**	In addition to the lagging indicator data for the applying level, school leaders regularly collect and analyze quick data like the following: • The administration reviews collaborative team common assessment and student achievement data-tracking documents and provides feedback to teams quarterly. • Collaborative team meetings and classroom observations indicate that all team members utilize common assessments at the same time. • Observations of collaborative team meetings indicate that teacher teams are utilizing common assessment student achievement data to design reteach opportunities for students who have not met proficiency on every priority standard. • In quick conversations, teachers can describe student proficiency on the assessed priority standards using their team's common assessments. If the data indicate current or potential problems, school leadership develops and executes plans to address these problems.
3 **Applying**	Systems and practices for monitoring progress toward school achievement goals have been established. 100 percent of collaborative teams establish and utilize common formative assessments for each priority standard or topic in their courses. 100 percent of collaborative teams establish and utilize student-data-tracking systems to track and report individual student proficiency on every priority standard or topic. 100 percent of collaborative teams utilize common assessment student achievement data to design reteach opportunities for students who have not met proficiency on every priority standard.
2 **Developing**	Systems and practices for monitoring progress toward school achievement goals have been established.
1 **Beginning**	Some systems and practices for monitoring progress toward school achievement goals have been established, even if those systems and practices are not complete.

Example Quick Data Sources

- Data-tracking sources are available to indicate progress toward schoolwide goals.
- When asked, teachers can discuss their students' progress toward schoolwide goals.
- Schoolwide goal-progress data are shared and discussed at leadership meetings and staff meetings.
- Artifacts of practice from collaborative teams indicate monitoring of student progress toward schoolwide achievement goals.

Leading Indicator 3.6

The school establishes appropriate school- and classroom-level programs and practices to help students meet individual achievement goals when data indicate interventions are needed.

Leadership Accountability Scale

Step	Status	Description	Directions
C	**4** **Sustaining**	The school cultivates data through quick data sources to monitor appropriate schoolwide and classroom intervention programs and practices to help students meet individual achievement goals, *and* it takes proper actions to intervene when quick data indicate a potential problem.	If yes, Sustaining If no, Applying
B	**3** **Applying**	The school has protocols and practices in place to ensure that appropriate schoolwide and classroom intervention programs and practices are used to help students meet individual achievement goals when data indicate interventions are needed, *and* can provide data and concrete artifacts of practice proving the desired effects of these actions.	If yes, go to step C If no, Developing
A	**2** **Developing**	The school has protocols and practices in place to ensure that appropriate schoolwide and classroom intervention programs and practices are used to help students meet individual achievement goals when data indicate interventions are needed.	If yes, go to step B If no, go to step D
D	**1** **Beginning**	The school is in the beginning, yet incomplete, stages of implementing schoolwide and classroom intervention programs and practices to help students meet individual achievement goals when data indicate interventions are needed.	If yes, Beginning If no, Not Attempting
	0 **Not Attempting**	The school has not attempted to implement schoolwide and classroom intervention programs and practices to help students meet individual achievement goals.	

Sample Lagging Indicators and Quick Data

Score	Sample Lagging Indicators With Concrete Criteria and Quantifiable Cut Scores
4 **Sustaining**	In addition to the lagging indicator data for the applying level, school leaders regularly collect and analyze quick data like the following: • The administration reviews collaborative team common assessment and student achievement data-tracking documents and provides feedback to teams quarterly. • Collaborative team meetings and classroom observations indicate that teachers give all students extra time and extra support to gain proficiency on or extend and enhance their understanding of priority standards. • Observations of collaborative team meetings indicate that teacher teams are designing reteach and enrichment opportunities for students on every priority standard. • In quick conversations, teachers can explain intervention and extension opportunities available to their students. • In surveys, 100 percent of students indicate that they are regularly given intervention and enrichment opportunities during the school day. If the data indicate current or potential problems, school leadership develops and executes plans to address these problems.
3 **Applying**	Protocols and practices are in place to ensure that appropriate schoolwide and classroom intervention programs and practices are used to help students meet individual achievement goals when data indicate interventions are needed. 100 percent of students will be given extra time and extra support during the school day to gain proficiency on each priority standard. 100 percent of students are given opportunities to extend or enhance their learning when data show they have met proficiency on priority standards. 100 percent of teachers include extra time and extra support opportunities for individual student proficiency on every priority standard or topic in their daily and unit plans. 100 percent of teachers engage in school schedules that provide students with extra time and extra support to gain proficiency on every priority standard or topic, as well as opportunities to extend or enhance student achievement.
2 **Developing**	Formal practices and protocols are in place to ensure that appropriate schoolwide and classroom intervention programs and practices are used to help students meet individual achievement goals when data indicate interventions are needed.
1 **Beginning**	Some practices and protocols are in place to ensure that appropriate schoolwide and classroom intervention programs and practices are used to help students meet individual achievement goals when data indicate interventions are needed, even if those practices and protocols are not complete.

Example Quick Data Sources

- Data sets indicate academic progress by groups of students served by schoolwide or classroom-level intervention programs.
- When asked, teachers can describe specific intervention strategies they are using.
- Collaborative team artifacts show the structure of team academic interventions and extensions.
- Quick discussions at staff meetings provide teachers opportunities to share how they are using classroom intervention strategies.
- Students can explain how schoolwide intervention time is designed to help them learn.

Level 4

At level 4 of the HRS framework, schools develop standards-referenced reporting.

Leading Indicator 4.1

The school establishes clear and measurable goals focused on critical needs regarding improving achievement of individual students.

Leadership Accountability Scale

Step	Status	Description	Directions
C	4 Sustaining	The school cultivates data through quick data sources to monitor the use of protocols and practices to ensure that clear and measurable goals are established and focused on critical needs regarding improving achievement of individual students, *and* it takes proper actions to intervene when quick data indicate a potential problem.	If yes, Sustaining If no, Applying
B	3 Applying	The school has protocols and practices in place to ensure that clear and measurable goals are established and focused on critical needs regarding improving achievement of individual students, *and* can produce lagging indicator data and concrete artifacts of practice proving the desired effects of these actions.	If yes, go to step C If no, Developing
A	2 Developing	The school has protocols and practices in place to ensure that clear and measurable goals are established and focused on critical needs regarding improving achievement of individual students.	If yes, go to step B If no, go to step D
D	1 Beginning	The school is in the beginning, yet incomplete, stages of implementing protocols and practices to ensure that clear and measurable goals are established and focused on critical needs regarding improving achievement of individual students.	If yes, Beginning If no, Not Attempting
	0 Not Attempting	The school has not attempted to implement protocols and practices to ensure that clear and measurable goals are established and focused on critical needs regarding improving achievement of individual students.	

Sample Lagging Indicators and Quick Data

Score	Sample Lagging Indicators With Concrete Criteria and Quantifiable Cut Scores
4 **Sustaining**	In addition to the lagging indicator data for the applying level, school leaders regularly collect and analyze quick data like the following: • Collaborative team meetings and classroom observations indicate that teachers have set individual student learning goals using proficiency scales. • Periodic reviews of student data notebooks show progress of student proficiency on learning goals. • In quick conversations, teachers can explain individual student status regarding their progress on specific learning goals. • In quick conversations, students can explain their status regarding their progress on specific learning goals. If the data indicate current or potential problems, school leadership develops and executes plans to address these problems.
3 **Applying**	Protocols and practices are in place to ensure that clear and measurable goals are established and focused on critical needs regarding improving achievement of individual students. 100 percent of students set goals using proficiency scales in at least one course or subject. 100 percent of students keep data notebooks and track their progress on learning goals. 100 percent of students participate in conferences focused on their individual progress of knowledge gain using proficiency scales. 100 percent of teacher teams establish written goals accompanied by proficiency scales for each student in terms of their knowledge gain.
2 **Developing**	Formal practices and protocols are in place to ensure that clear and measurable goals are established and focused on critical needs regarding improving achievement of individual students.
1 **Beginning**	Some practices and protocols are in place to ensure that clear and measurable goals are established and focused on critical needs regarding improving achievement of individual students, even if those practices and protocols are not complete.

Example Quick Data Sources

- Students can explain their individual achievement goals.
- Teachers can identify individual student achievement goals.
- Goal-setting formats indicate a student's individual goals.

Leading Indicator 4.2

The school analyzes, interprets, and uses data to regularly monitor progress toward achievement goals for individual students.

Leadership Accountability Scale

Step	Status	Description	Directions
C	4 Sustaining	The school cultivates information through quick data sources to monitor progress monitoring of individual student achievement goals, *and* it takes proper actions to intervene when quick data indicate a potential problem.	If yes, Sustaining If no, Applying
B	3 Applying	The school has established systems and practices for monitoring progress toward achievement goals for individual students, *and* can provide data and concrete artifacts of practice proving the desired effects of these actions.	If yes, go to step C If no, Developing
A	2 Developing	The school has established systems and practices for monitoring progress toward achievement goals for individual students.	If yes, go to step B If no, go to step D
D	1 Beginning	The school is in the beginning, yet incomplete, stages of establishing systems and practices for monitoring progress toward achievement goals for individual students.	If yes, Beginning If no, Not Attempting
	0 Not Attempting	The school has not attempted to establish systems and practices for monitoring progress toward achievement goals for individual students.	

Sample Lagging Indicators and Quick Data

Score	Sample Lagging Indicators With Concrete Criteria and Quantifiable Cut Scores
4 **Sustaining**	In addition to the lagging indicator data for the applying level, school leaders regularly collect and analyze quick data like the following: • Collaborative team meetings and classroom observations indicate that teachers monitor individual student learning goals using proficiency scales. • Periodic reviews of student data notebooks show progress of student proficiency on learning goals. • In quick conversations, teachers can explain individual student status regarding their progress on specific learning goals. • In quick conversations, students can explain their status regarding their progress on specific learning goals. If the data indicate current or potential problems, school leadership develops and executes plans to address these problems.
3 **Applying**	Protocols and practices are in place to ensure that data are analyzed and used to regularly monitor progress toward achievement goals for individual students. 100 percent of students monitor progress toward achievement of their goals using proficiency scales in at least one course or subject and individual student progress is shared with their parents. 100 percent of collaborative teams utilize student-data-tracking systems to monitor goals accompanied by proficiency scales for each individual student in terms of their knowledge gain. 100 percent of students are given opportunities to relearn or enhance their learning using proficiency scales.
2 **Developing**	Formal practices and protocols are in place to ensure that data are analyzed and used to regularly monitor progress toward achievement goals for individual students.
1 **Beginning**	Some practices and protocols are in place to ensure that data are analyzed and used to regularly monitor progress toward achievement goals for individual students, even if those practices and protocols are not complete.

Example Quick Data Sources

- Data-tracking sources are available to indicate progress toward individual student goals.
- When asked, teachers can discuss individual students' progress toward their achievement goals.
- Individual-student-goal-progress data are shared and discussed at leadership meetings and staff meetings.
- Artifacts of practice from collaborative teams indicate monitoring of student progress toward individual achievement goals.

Level 5

In level 5 of the HRS framework, schools develop competency-based education.

Leading Indicator 5.1

Students move on to the next level of the curriculum for any subject area only after they have demonstrated competence at the previous level.

Leadership Accountability Scale

Step	Status	Description	Directions
C	**4** **Sustaining**	The school cultivates information through quick data sources to monitor protocols and practices to ensure that students move on to the next curriculum level for any subject area only after they have demonstrated competence at the previous level, *and* it takes proper actions to intervene when quick data indicate a potential problem.	If yes, Sustaining If no, Applying
B	**3** **Applying**	The school has protocols and practices in place to ensure that students move on to the next curriculum level for any subject area only after they have demonstrated competence at the previous level, *and* can provide data and concrete artifacts of practice proving the desired effects of these actions.	If yes, go to step C If no, Developing
A	**2** **Developing**	The school has protocols and practices in place to ensure that students move on to the next curriculum level for any subject area only after they have demonstrated competence at the previous level.	If yes, go to step B If no, go to step D
D	**1** **Beginning**	The school is in the beginning, yet incomplete, stages of establishing protocols and practices to ensure that students move on to the next curriculum level for any subject area only after they have demonstrated competence at the previous level.	If yes, Beginning If no, Not Attempting
	0 **Not Attempting**	The school has not attempted to establish protocols and practices to ensure that students move on to the next curriculum level for any subject area only after they have demonstrated competence at the previous level.	

Sample Lagging Indicators and Quick Data

Score	Sample Lagging Indicators With Concrete Criteria and Quantifiable Cut Scores
4 **Sustaining**	In addition to the lagging indicator data for the applying level, school leaders regularly collect and analyze quick data like the following: • Collaborative teams and teachers track and report individual student competency levels. • Survey data indicate that parents can explain the system used to determine student competency. • In quick conversations, teachers can explain how they determine student competency for specific standards in a grade level or content area. • In quick conversations, students can explain their status regarding their progress in specific content areas using proficiency scales. If the data indicate current or potential problems, school leadership develops and executes plans to address these problems.
3 **Applying**	Protocols and practices are in place to ensure that students move on to the next curriculum level for any subject area only after they have demonstrated competence at the previous level. 100 percent of grade levels and courses have proficiency scales in place to clearly explain competency criteria for each priority standard or topic at each grade level. 100 percent of grade levels and courses clarify competency criteria using proficiency scales and share the criteria with students and their parents. 100 percent of student progress is tracked and reported using proficiency scales.
2 **Developing**	Formal practices and protocols are in place to ensure that students move on to the next curriculum level for any subject area only after they have demonstrated competence at the previous level.
1 **Beginning**	Some practices and protocols are in place to ensure that students move on to the next curriculum level for any subject area only after they have demonstrated competence at the previous level, even if those practices and protocols are not complete.

Example Quick Data Sources

- Tracking data indicate which students have mastered all content and moved to the next level.
- Students can explain their level of current study in each content area.

Leading Indicator 5.2

The school schedule accommodates students moving at a pace appropriate to their situation and needs.

Leadership Accountability Scale

Step	Status	Description	Directions
C	**4** **Sustaining**	The school cultivates information through quick data sources to monitor protocols and practices to ensure that the school's schedule is designed to accommodate students moving at a pace appropriate to their situation, *and* it takes proper actions to intervene when quick data indicate a potential problem.	If yes, Sustaining If no, Applying
B	**3** **Applying**	The school has protocols and practices in place to ensure that the school's schedule is designed to accommodate students moving at a pace appropriate to their situation and needs in all content areas, *and* can provide data and concrete artifacts of practice proving the desired effects of these actions.	If yes, go to step C If no, Developing
A	**2** **Developing**	The school has protocols and practices in place to ensure that the school's schedule is designed to accommodate students moving at a pace appropriate to their situation and needs in all content areas.	If yes, go to step B If no, go to step D
D	**1** **Beginning**	The school is in the beginning, yet incomplete, stages of establishing protocols and practices to ensure that the school's schedule is designed to accommodate students moving at a pace appropriate to their situation and needs in all content areas.	If yes, Beginning If no, Not Attempting
	0 **Not Attempting**	The school has not attempted to establish protocols and practices to ensure that the school's schedule is designed to accommodate students moving at a pace appropriate to their situation and needs in all content areas.	

Sample Lagging Indicators and Quick Data

Score	Sample Lagging Indicators With Concrete Criteria and Quantifiable Cut Scores
4 **Sustaining**	In addition to the lagging indicator data for the applying level, school leaders regularly collect and analyze quick data like the following: • Periodic focus groups with students and parents are conducted to ascertain the impact of competency-based schedules and systems on students' learning experience. • Collaborative teams and teachers track and report individual students moving at a pace appropriate to their own needs. • In quick conversations, teachers can explain how the school schedule is organized to accommodate individual student needs and progress. • In quick conversations, students can explain their use of individualized learning opportunities that allow them to move at a pace appropriate to their needs. If the data indicate current or potential problems, school leadership develops and executes plans to address these problems.
3 **Applying**	Protocols and practices are in place to ensure that the school schedule is designed to accommodate students moving at a pace appropriate to their situation and needs in all content areas. 100 percent of student schedules are built with pathways for vertical matriculation as competency is gained in different content areas. 100 percent of classroom observations indicate that students work at various learning levels to meet their individual needs in specific content areas. 100 percent of students have opportunities to engage in individualized learning opportunities at a pace appropriate for their own needs.
2 **Developing**	Formal practices and protocols are in place to ensure that the school schedule is designed to accommodate students moving at a pace appropriate to their situation and needs in all content areas.
1 **Beginning**	Some practices and protocols are in place to ensure that the school schedule is designed to accommodate students moving at a pace appropriate to their situation and needs in all content areas, even if those practices and protocols are not complete.

Example Quick Data Sources

- Periodic focus groups with students indicate the schedule is working to meet their needs to progress as learners.
- Data reports indicate students who have moved to the next level of learning when they were ready.
- Short surveys of teachers indicate the schedule allows students to move at a pace appropriate for their individual learning.

Leading Indicator 5.3

The school affords students who have demonstrated competency levels greater than those articulated in the system immediate opportunities to begin work on advanced content or career paths of interest.

Leadership Accountability Scale

Step	Status	Description	Directions
C	4 Sustaining	The school cultivates information through quick data sources to monitor protocols and practices to ensure that students who have demonstrated competency levels greater than those articulated in the system are afforded immediate opportunities to begin work on advanced content or career paths of interest, *and* it takes proper actions to intervene when quick data indicate a potential problem.	If yes, Sustaining If no, Applying
B	3 Applying	The school has protocols and practices in place to ensure that students who have demonstrated competency levels greater than those articulated in the system are afforded immediate opportunities to begin work on advanced content or career paths of interest, *and* can provide data and concrete artifacts of practice proving the desired effects of these actions.	If yes, go to step C If no, Developing
A	2 Developing	The school has protocols and practices in place to ensure that students who have demonstrated competency levels greater than those articulated in the system are afforded immediate opportunities to begin work on advanced content or career paths of interest.	If yes, go to step B If no, go to step D
D	1 Beginning	The school is in the beginning, yet incomplete, stages of establishing protocols and practices to ensure that students who have demonstrated competency levels greater than those articulated in the system are afforded immediate opportunities to begin work on advanced content or career paths of interest.	If yes, Beginning If no, Not Attempting
	0 Not Attempting	The school has not attempted to establish protocols and practices to ensure that students who have demonstrated competency levels greater than those articulated in the system are afforded immediate opportunities to begin work on advanced content or career paths of interest.	

Sample Lagging Indicators and Quick Data

Score	Sample Lagging Indicators With Concrete Criteria and Quantifiable Cut Scores
4 **Sustaining**	In addition to the lagging indicator data for the applying level, school leaders regularly collect and analyze quick data like the following: • Using surveys, parents can explain different options students access to work on advanced content and career interest pathways. • In quick conversations, students can explain different options they access to work on advanced content and career interest pathways. • The administration reviews data that show the percentage of students engaged in advanced and career interest pathway coursework to eliminate differences in advanced and career pathway opportunities for students of different socioeconomic levels, different learning needs, or differing ethnicities. If the data indicate current or potential problems, school leadership develops and executes plans to address these problems.
3 **Applying**	Protocols and practices are in place to ensure that students who have demonstrated competency levels greater than those articulated in the system are afforded immediate opportunities to begin work on advanced content or career paths of interest. 90 percent of students have opportunities to engage in coursework that leads to eventual college credit or industry certification. 100 percent of students have opportunities to engage in advanced content. 100 percent of students have opportunities to engage in career path interest studies.
2 **Developing**	Formal practices and protocols are in place to ensure that students who have demonstrated competency levels greater than those articulated in the system are afforded immediate opportunities to begin work on advanced content or career paths of interest.
1 **Beginning**	Some practices and protocols are in place to ensure that students who have demonstrated competency levels greater than those articulated in the system are afforded immediate opportunities to begin work on advanced content or career paths of interest, even if those practices and protocols are not complete.

Example Quick Data Sources

• Documents show options students have selected for career pathway opportunities.
• Academic records show advanced academic opportunities students are choosing.

References and Resources

ACT. (2023). *ACT technical manual*. Iowa City, IA: Author.

Adizes, I. (1990). *Managing corporate lifecycles*. Upper Saddle River, NJ: Prentice Hall.

Alabama State Department of Education. (n.d.). *Assessment*. Accessed at www.alabamaachieves.org/assessment/ on October 5, 2023.

Alaska Department of Education and Early Development. (n.d.). *Assessments*. Accessed at https://education.alaska.gov /assessments#c3gtabs-amp on June 6, 2023.

American Educational Research Association, American Psychological Association, & National Council on Measurement in Education. (2014). *The standards for educational and psychological testing*. Washington, DC: American Educational Research Association.

Anderson, J. R. (1976). *Language, memory, and thought*. Hillsdale, NJ: Erlbaum Associates.

Anderson, J. R. (1983). *The architecture of cognition*. Hillsdale, NJ: Erlbaum Associates.

Anderson, J. R. (1990). *The adaptive character of thought*. Hillsdale, NJ: Erlbaum Associates.

Anderson, J. R. (1993). *Rules of the mind*. Hillsdale, NJ: Erlbaum Associates.

Argyris, C., & Schön, D. A. (1974). *Theory in practice: Increasing professional effectiveness*. San Francisco: Jossey-Bass.

Argyris, C., & Schön, D. A. (1978). *Organizational learning: A theory of action perspective*. Reading, MA: Addison-Wesley.

Arizona Department of Education. (n.d.). *Welcome to assessments*. Accessed at www.azed.gov/assessment on September 22, 2023.

Arkansas Department of Education. (2023, January 17). *Assessment*. Accessed at https://dese.ade.arkansas.gov/ Offices/learning-services/assessment on September 22, 2023.

Bailey, K. D. (2008). Boundary maintenance in living systems theory and social entropy theory. *Systems Research and Behavioral Science, 25*(5), 587–597. https://doi.org/10.1002/sres.933

Bektaş, F., Çoğaltay, N., Karadağ, E., & Yusuf, A. (2015). School culture and academic achievement of students: A meta-analysis study. *The Anthropologist, 21*(3), 482–488.

Bellamy, G. T., Crawford, L., Marshall, L. H., & Coulter, G. A. (2005). The fail-safe schools challenge: Leadership possibilities from high reliability organizations. *Educational Administration Quarterly, 41*(3), 383–412.

Berman, A. I., Haertel, E. H., & Pellegrino, J. W. (2020). Introduction: Framing the issues. In A. I. Berman, E. H. Haertel, & J. W. Pellegrino (Eds.), *Comparability of large-scale educational assessments: Issues and recommendations* (pp. 9–24). Washington, DC: National Academy of Education.

Bierly, P. E., & Spender, J.-C. (1995). Culture and high reliability organizations: The case of the nuclear submarine. *Journal of Management, 21*(4), 639–656.

Bill & Melinda Gates Foundation. (2012). *Gathering feedback for teaching: Combining high-quality observations with student surveys and achievement gains* [Report]. Seattle, WA: Author. Accessed at https://usprogram.gatesfoundation .org/-/media/dataimport/resources/pdf/2016/12/met-gathering-feedback-research-paper1.pdf on May 5, 2023.

Bloom, B. S. (1984a). The search for methods of group instruction as effective as one-to-one tutoring. *Educational Leadership, 41*(8), 4–18.

Bloom, B. S. (1984b). The 2 sigma problem: The search for methods of group instruction as effective as one-to-one tutoring. *Educational Researcher, 13*(6), 4–16.

Borman, G. D., Hewes, G. M., Overman, L. T., & Brown, S. (2003). Comprehensive school reform and achievement: A meta-analysis. *Review of Educational Research, 73*(2), 125–230.

Bosker, R. J. (1992). *The stability and consistency of school effects in primary education.* Enschede, the Netherlands: University of Twente.

Bosker, R. J., & Witziers, B. (1995, January). *School effects, problems, solutions and a meta-analysis* [Conference presentation]. International Congress for School Effectiveness and Improvement, Leeuwarden, the Netherlands.

Bosker, R. J., & Witziers, B. (1996, April). *The magnitude of school effects. Or: Does it really matter which school a student attends?* [Conference presentation]. American Educational Research Association annual meeting, New York.

Brookhart, S. M., Guskey, T. R., Bowers, A. J., McMillan, J. H., Smith, J. K., Smith, L. F., et al. (2016). A century of grading research: Meaning and value in the most common educational measure. *Review of Educational Research, 86*(4), 803–848.

Brookover, W. B., Beady, C., Flood, P., Schweitzer, J., & Wisenbaker, J. (1979). *School social systems and student achievement: Schools can make a difference.* New York: Praeger.

Brookover, W. B., & Lezotte, L. W. (1979). *Changes in school characteristics coincident with changes in student achievement.* East Lansing, MI: Michigan State University.

Brookover, W. B., Schweitzer, J. H., Schneider, J. M., Beady, C. H., Flood, P. K., & Wisenbaker, J. M. (1978). Elementary school social climate and school achievement. *American Educational Research Journal, 15*(2), 301–318.

Buffum, A., Mattos, M., & Weber, C. (2009). *Pyramid response to intervention: RTI, professional learning communities, and how to respond when kids don't learn.* Bloomington, IN: Solution Tree Press.

California Department of Education. (2022). *Standardized testing and reporting (STAR).* Accessed at www.cde .ca.gov/re/pr/star.asp on June 6, 2023.

California Department of Education. (2023). *California assessment of student performance and progress (CAASPP) system.* Accessed at www.cde.ca.gov/ta/tg/ca/ on June 7, 2023.

Camilli, G., & Newton, P. E. (2022). Doing justice to fairness. In J. L. Jonson & K. F. Geisinger (Eds.), *Fairness in educational and psychological testing: Examining theoretical, research, practice, and policy implications of the 2014 standards* (pp. 111–130). Washington, DC: American Educational Research Association.

Chisholm, R. M. (1973). *The problem of the criterion.* Milwaukee, WI: Marquette University Press.

Cohen, J. (1960). A coefficient of agreement for nominal scales. *Educational and Psychological Measurement, 20*(1), 37–46.

Coleman, J. S., Campbell, E. Q., Hobson, C. J., McPartland, J., Mood, A. M., Weinfeld, F. D., et al. (1966). *Equality of educational opportunity.* Washington, DC: National Center for Educational Statistics.

The College Board. (2017). *SAT suite of assessments technical manual appendixes.* Iowa City, IA: Author.

Colorado Department of Education. (n.d.). *Assessment division.* Accessed at www.cde.state.co.us/assessment on June 6, 2023.

Connecticut State Department of Education. (n.d.). *Connecticut student assessment main page.* Accessed at https://portal.ct.gov/SDE/Student-Assessment/Main-Assessment/Student-Assessment on October 5, 2023.

Cronbach, L. J., & Meehl, P. E. (1955). Construct validity in psychological tests. *Psychological Bulletin, 52*(4), 281–302.

Cronbach, L. J., & Shavelson, R. J. (2004). My current thoughts on coefficient alpha and successor procedures. *Educational and Psychological Measurement, 64*(3), 391–418.

Datnow, A., Borman, G. D., Stringfield, S., Overman, L. T., & Costellano, M. (2003). Comprehensive school reform in culturally and linguistically diverse contexts: Implementation and outcomes from a four-year study. *Educational Evaluation and Policy Analysis, 25*(2), 142–170.

Davis, P. J. (2011). Entropy and society: Can the physical/mathematical notions of entropy be usefully imported into the social sphere? *Journal of Humanistic Mathematics, 1*(1), 119–136. Accessed at https://scholarship.claremont .edu/cgi/viewcontent.cgi?article=1008&context=jhm on May 5, 2023.

de Leeuw, J. (2004). Senior editor's introduction. In R. A. Berk, *Regression analysis: A constructive critique* (pp. xi–xv). Thousand Oaks, CA: SAGE.

Delaware Department of Education. (n.d.). *Delaware System of Student Assessment (DeSSA).* Accessed at www.doe .k12.de.us/domain/111 on October 5, 2023.

DePascale, C., & Gong, B. (2020). Comparability of individual students' scores on the "same test." In A. I. Berman, E. H. Haertel, & J. W. Pellegrino (Eds.), *Comparability of large-scale educational assessments: Issues and recommendations* (pp. 25–48). Washington, DC: National Academy of Education.

DuFour, R., DuFour, R., Eaker, R., Many, T. W., & Mattos, M. (2016). *Learning by doing: A handbook for Professional Learning Communities at Work* (3rd ed.). Bloomington, IN: Solution Tree Press.

DuFour, R., & Marzano, R. J. (2011). *Leaders of learning: How district, school, and classroom leaders improve student achievement.* Bloomington, IN: Solution Tree Press.

Duhigg, C. (2012). *The power of habit: Why we do what we do in life and business.* New York: Random House.

Eaker, R., & Marzano, R. J. (Eds.). (2020). *Professional Learning Communities at Work and High Reliability Schools: Cultures of continuous learning.* Bloomington, IN: Solution Tree Press.

Edmonds, R. (1979a). *A discussion of the literature and issues related to effective schooling.* Cambridge, MA: Center for Urban Studies, Harvard Graduate School of Education.

Edmonds, R. (1979b). Effective schools for the urban poor. *Educational Leadership, 37*(1), 15–24

Edmonds, R. (1979c). Some schools work and more can. *Social Policy, 9,* 28–32.

Edmonds, R. (1981a). Making public schools effective. *Social Policy, 12*(2), 56–60.

Edmonds, R. (1981b). *The search for effective schools: The identification and analysis of city schools that are instructionally effective for poor children* [Unpublished report]. East Lansing, MI: Michigan State University.

Edmonds, R. R., & Frederiksen, J. R. (1979). *Search for effective schools: The identification and analysis of city schools that are instructionally effective for poor children.* Accessed at https://files.eric.ed.gov/fulltext/ED170396.pdf on May 5, 2023.

Elmore, R. F. (2003). *Knowing the right thing to do: School improvement and performance-based accountability.* Washington, DC: National Governors Association Center for Best Practices. Accessed at http://www.brjonesphd .com/uploads/1/6/9/4/16946150/0803knowing.pdf on July 26, 2023.

Equity. (n.d.). In *Dictionary.com.* Accessed at www.dictionary.com/browse/equity on July 13, 2023.

Ertmer, P. A. (1999). Addressing first- and second-order barriers to change: Strategies for technology integration. *Educational Technology Research and Development, 47*(4), 47–61.

Every Student Succeeds Act of 2015, Pub. L. No. 114-95, 20 U.S.C. § 1177 (2015).

Florida Department of Education. (n.d.a). *K–12 student assessment.* Accessed at www.fldoe.org/accountability /assessments/k-12-student-assessment/fsa.stml on June 6, 2023.

Florida Department of Education. (n.d.b). *Welcome to the Florida statewide assessments portal.* Accessed at https://flfast.org/index.html on June 6, 2023.

Fraser, B. J., Walberg, H. J., Welch, W. W., & Hattie, J. A. (1987). Syntheses of educational productivity research. *International Journal of Educational Research, 11*(2), 147–252.

Frisbie, D. A. (1988). Reliability of scores from teacher-made tests. *Educational Measurement: Issues and Practice, 7*(1), 25–35.

Garrett, H. E. (1937). *Statistics in psychology and education* (2nd ed.). New York: Longmans, Green.

Gawande, A. (2007). *Better: A surgeon's notes on performance.* New York: Metropolitan Books.

Gawande, A. (2009). *The checklist manifesto: How to get things right.* New York: Metropolitan Books.

Georgia Department of Education. (n.d.a). *Georgia milestones assessment system.* Accessed at www.gadoe.org/ Curriculum-Instruction-and-Assessment/Assessment/Pages/Georgia-Milestones-Assessment-System.aspx on June 6, 2023.

Georgia Department of Education. (n.d.b). *Retired: Criterion-referenced competency tests (CRCT).* Accessed at www.gadoe.org/Curriculum-Instruction-and-Assessment/Assessment/Pages/CRCT.aspx on June 6, 2023.

Georgia Department of Education. (n.d.c). *Retired: Georgia alternate assessment (GAA).* Accessed at www.gadoe .org/Curriculum-Instruction-and-Assessment/Assessment/Pages/GAA.aspx on June 6, 2023.

Georgia Department of Education. (n.d.d). *Retired: Georgia high school graduation tests (GHSGT).* Accessed at www.gadoe.org/Curriculum-Instruction-and-Assessment/Assessment/Pages/GHSGT.aspx on June 6, 2023.

Georgia Department of Education. (n.d.e). *Writing assessments.* Accessed at www.gadoe.org/Curriculum -Instruction-and-Assessment/Assessment/Pages/Writing-Assessments.aspx on June 6, 2023.

Glaser, J. E. (2017, March 20). The caring effect: Celebrate and reward good efforts. *Psychology Today.* Accessed at www. psychologytoday.com/us/blog/conversational-intelligence/201703/the-caring-effect on March 10, 2023.

Glaser, R., & Linn, R. (1993). Foreword. In L. Shepard, *Setting performance standards for student achievement* (pp. xiii-xiv). Stanford, CA: National Academy of Education, Stanford University.

Glass, G. V., McGaw, B., & Smith, M. L. (1981). *Meta-analysis in social research.* Beverly Hills, CA: SAGE.

Glenn, B. C., & McLean, T. (1981). *What works? An examination of effective schools for poor Black children.* Cambridge, MA: Harvard Center for Law and Education.

Guilford, J. P. (1946). New standards for test evaluation. *Educational and Psychological Measurement, 6*(4), 427–438.

Hall, G. E., & Hord, S. M. (1987). *Change in schools: Facilitating the process.* Albany, NY: State University of New York Press.

Hall, G. E., Loucks, S. F., Rutherford, W. L., & Newlove, B. W. (1975). Levels of use of the innovation: A framework for analyzing innovation adoption. *Journal of Teacher Education, 26*(1), 52–56.

Handy, C. (1995). *The empty raincoat: Making sense of the future.* New York: Random House.

Hathcoat, J. D. (2013). Validity semantics in educational and psychological assessment. *Practical Assessment, Research, and Evaluation, 18*(9), 1–14.

Hattie, J. (1992). Measuring the effects of schooling. *Australian Journal of Education, 36*(1), 5–13.

Hattie, J. (2009). *Visible learning: A synthesis of over 800 meta-analyses relating to achievement.* New York: Routledge.

Hattie, J. (2012). *Visible learning for teachers: Maximizing impact on learning.* New York: Routledge.

Hattie, J. (2015). The applicability of Visible Learning to higher education. *Scholarship of Teaching and Learning in Psychology, 1*(1), 79–91.

Hattie, J., Biggs, J., & Purdie, N. (1996). Effects of learning skills interventions on student learning: A meta-analysis. *Review of Educational Research, 66*(2), 99–136.

Hawaii State Department of Education. (n.d.). *Testing.* Accessed at www.hawaiipublicschools.org/TeachingAndLearning/Testing/Pages/home.aspx on October 5, 2023.

Haystead, M. W. (2015). *Reliability analysis report.* Centennial, CO: Marzano Resources.

Haystead, M. W., & Marzano, R. J. (2022). *A validity study of GLEs as predictors of student performance on external assessments: Preliminary analysis.* Centennial, CO: Marzano Academies.

Heifetz, R. A. (1994). *Leadership without easy answers.* Cambridge, MA: Harvard University Press.

Herman, R., Aladjem, D., McMahon, P., Masem, E., Mulligan, I., O'Malley, A., et al. (1999). *An educators' guide to schoolwide reform.* Washington, DC: American Institutes for Research.

Hipkins, R., & Cowie, B. (2016). The sigmoid curve as a metaphor for growth and change. *Teachers and Curriculum, 16*(2). Accessed at https://files.eric.ed.gov/fulltext/EJ1123357.pdf on June 6, 2023.

Hord, S. M., Rutherford, W. L., Huling-Austin, L., & Hall, G. E. (1987). *Taking charge of change.* Alexandria, VA: ASCD.

Idaho State Department of Education. (n.d.). *Assessment & accountability.* Accessed at www.sde.idaho.gov/assessment on June 6, 2023.

Illinois State Board of Education. (n.d.). *Assessment.* Accessed at www.isbe.net/Pages/Assessment.aspx on October 5, 2023.

Indiana Department of Education. (2023). *2023 Indiana academic standards: Mathematics—Grade 5.* Accessed at https://media.doe.in.gov/standards/indiana-academic-standards-grade-5-mathematics.pdf on July 11, 2023.

Indiana Department of Education. (n.d.). *Assessment.* Accessed at www.in.gov/doe/students/assessment/ on October 5, 2023.

Iowa Department of Education. (n.d.). *Student assessment (PK–12).* Accessed at https://educateiowa.gov/pk-12/student-assessment-pk-12 on October 5, 2023.

Jencks, C., Smith, M., Acland, H., Bane, M. J., Cohen, D., Gintis, H., et al. (1972). *Inequality: A reassessment of the effect of family and schooling in America.* New York: Basic Books.

Jordan, V. B., & Brownlee, L. (1981, April 13–17). *Meta-analysis of the relationship between Piagetian and school achievement tests* [Conference presentation]. American Educational Research Association annual meeting, Los Angeles.

Kane, M. T. (1992). An argument-based approach to validity. *Psychological Bulletin, 112*(3), 527–535.

Kane, M. T. (2001). Current concerns in validity theory. *Journal of Educational Measurement, 38*(4), 319–342.

Kane, M. T. (2009). Validating the interpretations and uses of test scores. In R. W. Lissitz (Ed.), *The concept of validity: Revisions, new directions, and applications* (pp. 39–64). Charlotte, NC: Information Age.

Kansas State Department of Education. (n.d.). *Assessments.* Accessed at www.ksde.org/Agency/Division-of-Learning-Services/Career-Standards-and-Assessment-Services/CSAS-Home/Assessments on June 6, 2023.

Keng, L., & Marion, S. (2020). Comparability of aggregated group scores on the "same test." In A. I. Berman, E. H. Haertel, & J. W. Pellegrino (Eds.), *Comparability of large-scale educational assessments: Issues and recommendations* (pp. 49–74). Washington, DC: National Academy of Education.

Kentucky Department of Education. (2023, July 28). *Assessments.* Accessed at https://education.ky.gov/AA/Assessments/Pages/default.aspx on October 5, 2023.

Klitgaard, R. E., & Hall, G. R. (1975). Are there unusually effective schools? *Journal of Human Resources, 10*(1), 90–106.

Kosena, B. J., & Marzano, R. J. (2022). *Attaining competency-based education (part 1)* [Webinar]. Accessed at www.marzanoresources.com/attaining-competency-based-education-part-1-webinar.html on May 5, 2023.

Lehman, E., De Jong, D., & Baron, M. (2018). Investigating the relationship of standards-based grades vs. traditional-based grades to results of the Scholastic Math Inventory at the middle school level. *Education Leadership Review of Doctoral Research, 6,* 1–16.

Lezotte, L. W. (1989). School improvement based on the effective schools research. *International Journal of Educational Research, 13*(7), 815–825.

Lipsey, M. W., Puzio, K., Yun, C., Hebert, M. A., Steinka-Fry, K., Cole, M. W., et al. (2012, November). *Translating the statistical representation of the effects of education interventions into more readily interpretable forms.* Washington, DC: U.S. Department of Education.

Lipsey, M. W., & Wilson, D. B. (1993). The efficacy of psychological, educational, and behavioral treatment: Confirmation from meta-analysis. *American Psychologist, 48*(12), 1181–1209.

Louisiana Department of Education. (n.d.). *Assessments.* Accessed at www.louisianabelieves.com/resources/search/assessment on October 5, 2023.

Mace, R. (1985). Universal design: Barrier-free environments for everyone. *Designers West, 33*(1), 147–152.

Madaus, G. F., Airasian, P. W., & Kellaghan, T. (1980). *School effectiveness: A reassessment of the evidence.* New York: McGraw-Hill.

Maine Department of Education. (n.d.). *Maine comprehensive assessment system (MECAS).* Accessed at www.maine.gov/doe/Testing_Accountability/MECAS on June 6, 2023.

Martínez-Berumen, H. A., López-Torres, G. C., & Romo-Rojas, L. (2014). Developing a method to evaluate entropy in organizational systems. *Procedia Computer Science, 28,* 389–397. https://doi.org/10.1016/j.procs.2014.03.048

Maryland State Department of Education. (n.d.). *Assessments.* Accessed at https://marylandpublicschools.org/about/Pages/DAAIT/Assessment/index.aspx on October 5, 2023.

Marzano, R. J. (2001). *A new era of school reform: Going where the research takes us.* Aurora, CO: Mid-Continent Research for Education and Learning.

Marzano, R. J. (2003). *What works in schools: Translating research into action.* Alexandria, VA: ASCD.

Marzano, R. J. (2010). *Formative assessment and standards-based grading.* Bloomington, IN: Marzano Resources.

Marzano, R. J. (2013). *Becoming a High Reliability School: The next step in school reform.* Centennial, CO: Marzano Resources.

Marzano, R. J. (2017). *The new art and science of teaching.* Bloomington, IN: Solution Tree Press.

Marzano, R. J. (2018). *Making classroom assessments reliable and valid.* Bloomington, IN: Solution Tree Press.

Marzano, R. J. (2021). *Guidelines for cumulative review.* Centennial, CO: Marzano Academies.

Marzano, R. J., Dodson, C. W., Simms, J. A., & Wipf, J. P. (2022). *Ethical test preparation in the classroom.* Bloomington, IN: Marzano Resources.

Marzano, R. J., & Eaker, R. (2020). Professional Learning Communities at Work and High Reliability Schools: Merging best practices for school improvement. In R. Eaker & R. J. Marzano (Eds.), *Professional Learning Communities at Work and High Reliability Schools: Cultures of continuous learning* (pp. 1–30). Bloomington, IN: Solution Tree Press.

Marzano, R. J., & Hardy, P. B. (2023). *Leading a competency-based secondary school: The Marzano Academies model.* Bloomington, IN: Marzano Resources.

Marzano, R. J., & Haystead, M. W. (2022). *A validity study of GLEs as predictors of student performance on external assessments: Final analysis.* Centennial, CO: Marzano Academies.

Marzano, R. J., & Haystead, M. W. (2023). *A validity study of GLEs as predictors of student performance on external assessments: Secondary analysis.* Centennial, CO: Marzano Academies.

Marzano, R. J., & Kendall, J. S. (1996). *A comprehensive guide to designing standards-based districts, schools, and classrooms.* Alexandria, VA: ASCD.

Marzano, R. J., & Kosena, B. J. (2022). *Leading a competency-based elementary school: The Marzano Academies model.* Bloomington, IN: Marzano Resources.

Marzano, R. J., Norford, J. S., Finn, M., & Finn, D., III. (2017). *A handbook for personalized competency-based education.* Bloomington, IN: Marzano Resources.

Marzano, R. J., Norford, J. S., & Ruyle, M. (2019). *The new art and science of classroom assessment.* Bloomington, IN: Solution Tree Press.

Marzano, R. J., Rains, C. L., & Warrick, P. B. (2021). *Improving teacher development and evaluation: A guide for leaders, coaches, and teachers.* Bloomington, IN: Marzano Resources.

Marzano, R. J., Warrick, P. B., Rains, C. L., & DuFour, R. (2018). *Leading a High Reliability School.* Bloomington, IN: Solution Tree Press.

Marzano, R. J., Warrick, P. B., & Simms, J. A. (2014). *A handbook for High Reliability Schools: The next step in school reform.* Bloomington, IN: Marzano Resources.

Marzano, R. J., & Waters, T. (2009). *District leadership that works: Striking the right balance.* Bloomington, IN: Solution Tree Press.

Marzano, R. J., Waters, T., & McNulty, B. A. (2005). *School leadership that works: From research to results.* Alexandria, VA: ASCD.

Marzano, R. J., Yanoski, D. C., Hoegh, J. K., & Simms, J. A. (2013). *Using Common Core standards to enhance classroom instruction and assessment.* Bloomington, IN: Marzano Resources.

Massachusetts Department of Elementary and Secondary Education. (2023, October 3). *Massachusetts comprehensive assessment system.* Accessed at www.doe.mass.edu/mcas/default.html on October 5, 2023.

Mavrofides, T., Kameas, A., Papageorgiou, D., & Los, A. (2011). On the entropy of social systems: A revision of the concepts of entropy and energy in the social context. *Systems Research and Behavioral Science.* Accessed at https://eeyem.eap.gr/wp-content/uploads/2017/06/17.On-the-Entropy-of-Social-Systems-A-Revision-of-the-Concepts-of-Entropy-and-Energy-in-the-Social-Context-.pdf on March 3, 2023.

Merit Software. (2015). *The Oklahoma core curriculum tests (OCCT).* Accessed at https://web.archive.org/web/20160306122830/https://www.meritsoftware.com/standardized_tests/OK.php on June 7, 2023.

Messick, S. (1975). The standard problem: Meaning and values in measurement and evaluation. *American Psychologist, 30*(10), 955–966.

Messick, S. (1993). Validity. In R. L. Linn (Ed.), *Educational measurement* (3rd ed., pp. 13–104). Phoenix, AZ: Oryx Press.

Metwaly, A. M., Ghoneim, M. M., Eissa, I. H., Elsehemy, I. A., Mostafa, A. E., Hegazy, M. M., et al. (2021). Traditional ancient Egyptian medicine: A review. *Saudi Journal of Biological Sciences, 28*(10), 5823–5832. Accessed at www.sciencedirect.com/science/article/pii/S1319562X21005027 on August 4, 2023.

Michigan Department of Education. (n.d.). *M-STEP summative.* Accessed at www.michigan.gov/mde/Services/Student-Assessment/m-step on June 6, 2023.

Mid-Continent Research for Education and Learning. (2014). *Content knowledge: Online edition—Browse the online edition standards and benchmarks.* Accessed at www2.mcrel.org/compendium/browse.asp on May 3, 2018.

Minnesota Department of Education. (n.d.). *Statewide testing.* Accessed at https://education.mn.gov/mde/fam/tests/ on October 5, 2023.

Mississippi Department of Education. (n.d.). *Student assessment*. Accessed at www.mdek12.org/OSA on October 5, 2023.

Missouri Department of Elementary and Secondary Education. (n.d.). *Assessment*. Accessed at https://dese.mo.gov/quality-schools/assessment on October 5, 2023.

Montana Office of Public Instruction. (n.d.). *Montana comprehensive assessment system*. Accessed at https://opi.mt.gov/Leadership/Assessment-Accountability/MontCAS on June 6, 2023.

Mosteller, F., & Moynihan, D. P. (1972). A pathbreaking report. In F. Mosteller & D. P. Moynihan (Eds.), *On equality of educational opportunity* (pp. 3–68). New York: Vintage Books.

Muhammad, A. (2015). *Overcoming the achievement gap trap: Liberating mindsets to effect change*. Bloomington, IN: Solution Tree Press.

National Center for Education Evaluation and Regional Assistance. (n.d.). *Search results*. Accessed at https://ies.ed.gov/ncee/wwc/Search/Products?productType=1 on July 12, 2023.

National Governors Association Center for Best Practices & Council of Chief State School Officers. (2010a). *Common Core State Standards for English language arts and literacy in history/social studies, science, and technical subjects*. Washington, DC: Authors.

National Governors Association Center for Best Practices & Council of Chief State School Officers. (2010b). *Common Core State Standards for mathematics*. Washington, DC: Authors.

National Governors Association Center for Best Practices & Council of Chief State School Officers. (2010c). *Reaching higher: The Common Core State Standards validation committee*. Washington, DC: Authors.

National Governors Association Center for Best Practices & Council of Chief State School Officers. (n.d.a). *Common Core State Standards for English language arts and literacy in history/social studies, science, and technical subjects: Appendix A—Research supporting key elements of the standards*. Washington, DC: Authors.

National Governors Association Center for Best Practices & Council of Chief State School Officers. (n.d.b). *Common Core State Standards for English language arts and literacy in history/social studies, science, and technical subjects: Appendix B—Text exemplars and sample performance tasks*. Washington, DC: Authors.

Nebraska Department of Education. (2023, August 4). *NSCAS overview*. Accessed at www.education.ne.gov/assessment/nscas-system/ on August 10, 2023.

Nevada Department of Education. (n.d.). *Assessment*. Accessed at https://doe.nv.gov/Assessments/ on June 6, 2023.

New Hampshire Department of Education. (n.d.). *New Hampshire statewide assessment system*. Accessed at www.education.nh.gov/who-we-are/division-of-learner-support/bureau-of-instructional-support/office-of-assessment/statewide-assessement-system on September 26, 2023.

New Jersey Department of Education. (n.d.). Assessment. Accessed at www.nj.gov/education/assessment/index.shtml on October 5, 2023.

New Mexico Public Education Department. (2023, August 18). *Assessment*. Accessed at https://webnew.ped.state.nm.us/bureaus/assessment/ on October 5, 2023.

New York State Education Department. (n.d.a). *Accommodations for testing*. Accessed at www.nysed.gov/state-assessment/accommodations-testing on June 6, 2023.

New York State Education Department. (n.d.b). *State assessment*. Accessed at www.nysed.gov/state-assessment on June 6, 2023.

NGSS Lead States. (2013). *Next Generation Science Standards: For states, by states*. Washington, DC: National Academies Press.

North Carolina Department of Public Instruction. (n.d.). *State tests*. Accessed at www.dpi.nc.gov/districts-schools/testing-and-school-accountability/state-tests on October 5, 2023.

North Dakota Department of Public Instruction. (n.d.). *Assessment*. Accessed at www.nd.gov/dpi/districts schools/assessment on June 6, 2023.

Northwest Regional Educational Laboratory. (2000). *Catalog of school reform models* (2nd ed.). Portland, OR: Author.

Office of the State Superintendent of Education. (n.d.). *The partnership for assessment of readiness for college and careers (PARCC)*. Accessed at https://osse.dc.gov/parcc on June 6, 2023.

Ohio Department of Education. (n.d.). *Testing*. Accessed at https://education.ohio.gov/Topics/Testing on September 26, 2023.

Oklahoma State Department of Education. (2023, September 26). *Office of Assessments*. Accessed at www.dpi.nc.gov /districts-schools/testing-and-school-accountability/state-tests on October 5, 2023.

Oregon Department of Education. (n.d.). *Statewide assessments*. Accessed at www.oregon.gov/ode/educator-resources /assessment/Pages/Statewide-Assessments.aspx on September 26, 2023.

Pennsylvania Department of Education. (n.d.). *Assessment and accountability*. Accessed at www.education.pa.gov/K-12 /Assessment%20and%20Accountability/Pages/default.aspx on October 5, 2023.

Perrow, C. (1984). *Normal accidents: Living with high-risk technologies*. New York: Basic Books.

Preiser, W. F. E., & Smith, K. H. (2011). *Universal design handbook* (2nd ed.). New York: McGraw-Hill.

Purkey, S. C., & Smith, M. S. (1982). *Effective schools: A review*. Madison, WI: University of Wisconsin.

Purkey, S. C., & Smith, M. S. (1983). Effective schools: A review. *The Elementary School Journal*, *83*(4), 426–452.

Rains, C. L. (2020). Leadership in high reliability school districts. In R. Eaker & R. J. Marzano (Eds.), *Professional Learning Communities at Work and High Reliability Schools: Cultures of continuous learning* (pp. 351–383). Bloomington, IN: Solution Tree Press.

REL Midwest. (2019). *ESSA tiers of evidence: What you need to know* [Handout]. Accessed at https://ies.ed.gov/ncee /edlabs/regions/midwest/pdf/blogs/RELMW-ESSA-Tiers-Video-Handout-508.pdf on March 28, 2023.

Reynolds, D., & Teddlie, C. (2000). Linking school effectiveness and school improvement. In C. Teddlie & D. Reynolds (Eds.), *The international handbook of school effectiveness research* (pp. 206–231). New York: Routledge.

Rhode Island Department of Education. (n.d.a). *RICAS assessments*. Accessed at https://ride.ri.gov/instruction -assessment/assessment/ricas-assessments on June 7, 2023.

Rhode Island Department of Education. (n.d.b). *RICAS resource center*. Accessed at http://ricas.pearsonsupport.com on June 7, 2023.

Riehl, C. (2006). Feeling better: A comparison of medical research and education research. *Educational Researcher*, *35*(5), 24–29.

Roberts, K. H. (1990). Some characteristics of one type of high reliability organization. *Organization Science*, *1*(2), 160–176.

Rogers, E. M. (2003). *Diffusion of innovations* (5th ed.). New York: Free Press.

Rutter, M., Maughan, B., Mortimore, P., & Ouston, J. (1979). *Fifteen thousand hours: Secondary schools and their effects on children*. Cambridge, MA: Harvard University Press.

Scheerens, J. (1992). *Effective schooling: Research, theory and practice*. London: Cassell.

Scheerens, J., & Bosker, R. J. (1997). *The foundations of educational effectiveness*. New York: Pergamon.

Schneider, C., & Paul, J. (2015, September 16). Education chief Arne Duncan: U.S. is falling behind. *Indianapolis Star*. Accessed at www.indystar.com/story/news/politics/2015/09/16/education-chief-arne-duncan-us-falling -behind/32533827 on July 27, 2023.

Simms, J. A. (2016, August). *The critical concepts*. Centennial, CO: Marzano Resources. Accessed at www.marzano resources.com/the-critical-concepts.html on August 11, 2023.

Slanski, K. E. (2012). The law of Hammurabi and its audience. *Yale Journal of Law and the Humanities, 24*, 97–110.

South Carolina Department of Education. (n.d.). *Assessment information.* Accessed at https://ed.sc.gov/tests /assessment-information/ on October 5, 2023.

South Dakota Department of Education. (n.d.). *Office of Assessment.* Accessed at https://doe.sd.gov/assessment/ on October 5, 2023.

Spector, P. E. (1992). *Summated rating scale construction* (Sage University Paper series on Quantitative Applications in the Social Sciences, No. 07-082). Newbury Park, CA: SAGE.

Stringfield, S. (1995). Attempting to enhance students' learning through innovative programs: The case for schools evolving into high reliability organizations. *School Effectiveness and School Improvement, 6*(1), 67–96.

Tennessee Department of Education. (n.d.). *Tennessee comprehensive assessment program.* Accessed at www.tn.gov /education/districts/lea-operations/assessment/tnready.html on October 5, 2023.

Texas Education Agency. (n.d.). *STAAR resources.* Accessed at https://tea.texas.gov/student-assessment/testing/staar /staar-resources on October 5, 2023.

Thorndike, E. L. (1904). *An introduction to the theory of mental and social measurements.* New York: Science Press.

Todd, T. W. (1921). Egyptian medicine: A critical study of recent claims. *American Anthropologist, 23*(4), 460–470.

Torlakson, T., & Kirst, M. W. (2016, January 13). *Every Student Succeeds Act* [Letter to U.S. Department of Education]. Sacramento: California Department of Education. Accessed at https://www.cde.ca.gov/re/es /regletter1.asp on August 10, 2023.

U.S. Department of Education. (2002). *Comprehensive school reform (CSR) program guidance.* Accessed at www2.ed.gov/programs/compreform/guidance/guidance2002.pdf on July 13, 2023.

U.S. Department of Education. (n.d.). *Every Student Succeeds Act (ESSA).* Accessed at www.ed.gov/essa?src=rn%20 Retrieved%20August%203,%202017 on October 11, 2017.

U.S. Government. (2022, December 27). *Elementary and Secondary Education Act of 1965* [Amended through P. L. 117–286, enacted December 27, 2022]. Washington, DC: Author.

Utah State Board of Education. (n.d.). *Assessments.* Accessed at https://schools.utah.gov/assessment/assessments on October 5, 2023.

Venezky, R. L., & Winfield, L. F. (1979). *Schools that succeed beyond expectations in teaching* (Studies in education technical report no. 1). Newark: University of Delaware.

Vermont Agency of Education. (n.d.). *State and local assessments.* Accessed at https://education.vermont.gov/student -learning/assessments/state-and-local-assessments on October 5, 2023.

Virgina Department of Education. (n.d.). *Virginia SOL assessment program.* Accessed at www.doe.virginia.gov /teaching-learning-assessment/student-assessment/virginia-sol-assessment-program on October 5, 2023.

Walberg, H. J. (1980). *A psychological theory of educational productivity.* Washington, DC: National Institute of Education.

Walberg, H. J. (1984). Improving the productivity of America's schools. *Educational Leadership, 41*(8), 19–27.

Wang, M. C., Haertel, G. D., & Walberg, H. J. (1993). Toward a knowledge base for school learning. *Review of Educational Research, 63*(3), 249–294.

Warrick, P. B. (2020). High reliability leadership. In R. Eaker & R. J. Marzano (Eds.), *Professional Learning Communities at Work and High Reliability Schools: Cultures of continuous learning* (pp. 307–327). Bloomington, IN: Solution Tree Press.

Washington Office of Superintendent of Public Instruction. (n.d.). *State testing.* Accessed at https://ospi.k12.wa.us /student-success/testing/state-testing on October 5, 2023.

Waters, T., & Cameron, G. (2007). *The balanced leadership framework: Connecting vision with action.* Denver, CO: McREL.

Weaver, A. (2023, March 9). *An introduction to competency-based education with students and school leaders.* Accessed at https://aurora-institute.org/cw_post/recap-of-an-introduction-to-k-12-competency-based-education-webinar on June 27, 2023.

Weber, G. (1971). *Inner-city children can be taught to read: Four successful schools* (CBE occasional papers no. 18). Washington, DC: Council for Basic Education.

Weick, K. E., Sutcliffe, K. M., & Obstfeld, D. (1999). Organizing for high reliability: Processes of collective mindfulness. In R. I. Sutton & B. M. Staw (Eds.), *Research in organizational behavior* (Vol. 21, pp. 81–123). Greenwich, CT: JAI Press.

West Virginia Department of Education. (n.d.). *West Virginia general summative assessment (3–8).* Accessed at https://wvde.us/assessment/west-virginia-general-summative-assessment-3-8/ on June 7, 2023.

Wiggins, G. (1993, November). Assessment: Authenticity, context, and validity. *Phi Delta Kappan, 75*(3), 200–214.

Wiggins, G. (1996). Honesty and fairness: Toward better grading and reporting. In T. R. Guskey (Ed.), *ASCD yearbook, 1996: Communicating student learning* (pp. 141–177). Alexandria, VA: ASCD.

Williams, J. E. (n.d.). *How to sound out words.* Accessed at https://weallcanread.com/how-to-sound-out-words/ on October 7, 2021.

Willms, J. D. (1992). *Monitoring school performance: A guide for educators.* Washington, DC: Falmer Press.

Wisconsin Department of Public Instruction. (n.d.). *Assessment in Wisconsin.* Accessed at https://dpi.wi.gov /assessment on October 5, 2023.

Witkin, S. (2014). Change and deeper change: Transforming social work education. *Journal of Social Work Education, 50*(4), 587–598.

Wood, T. W. (2017). *Does the What Works Clearinghouse really work? Investigations into issues of policy, practice, and transparency.* Eugene, OR: National Institute for Direct Instruction.

Wyoming Department of Education. (n.d.). *Assessment—State system.* Accessed at https://edu.wyoming.gov/for -district-leadership/state-assessment/ on September 26, 2023.

Index

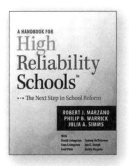

A Handbook for High Reliability Schools
Robert J. Marzano, Philip B. Warrick, and Julia A. Simms
Transform your schools into organizations that take proactive steps to ensure student success. Using a research-based, five-level hierarchy along with leading and lagging indicators, you'll learn to assess, monitor, and confirm the effectiveness of your schools.
BKL020

Leading a High Reliability School
Robert J. Marzano, Philip B. Warrick, Cameron L. Rains, and Richard DuFour
Learn how and why High Reliability Schools use interdependent systems of operation and the PLC at Work process to establish and maintain school effectiveness.
BKF795

Marzano Academies Series
The Marzano Academies series presents a blueprint for success with competency-based education from experts and educators who have done this work. Leaders and teachers at the elementary and secondary levels will gain innovative, equitable, and effective practices for schools and classrooms.
BKL056, BKL055, BKL053, BKL054

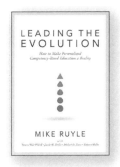

Leading the Evolution
Mike Ruyle with Tamera Weir O'Neill, Jeanie M. Iberlin, Michael D. Evans, and Rebecca Midles
Take action to evolve the existing model of schooling into one that is more innovative, relevant, and effective. *Leading the Evolution* introduces a three-pronged approach to driving substantive change—called the evolutionary triad—that connects transformational leadership, student engagement, and teacher optimism around personalized competency-based education.
BKL042

Leading Standards-Based Learning
Tammy Heflebower, Jan K. Hoegh, and Philip B. Warrick
Standards-based learning is a great step forward for schools, but it must be implemented correctly to ensure the best educational experience possible. In this comprehensive implementation guide, the authors outline a research-backed, five-phase plan for leading the transition to a standards-based system.
BKL052

MARZANO Resources   Visit MarzanoResources.com or call 888.849.0851 to order.

Professional Development
Designed for Success

Empower your staff to tap into their full potential as educators. As an all-inclusive research-into-practice resource center, we are committed to helping your school or district become highly effective at preparing every student for his or her future.

Choose from our wide range of customized professional development opportunities for teachers, administrators, and district leaders. Each session offers hands-on support, personalized answers, and accessible strategies that can be put into practice immediately.

Bring Marzano Resources experts to your school for results-oriented training on:

- ▶ Assessment & Grading
- ▶ Curriculum
- ▶ Instruction
- ▶ School Leadership
- ▶ Teacher Effectiveness
- ▶ Student Engagement
- ▶ Vocabulary
- ▶ Competency-Based Education

LEARN MORE at MarzanoResources.com/PD